Handcrafted Journals, Albums, Scrapbooks

& More

Handcrafted Journals, Albums, Scrapbooks

& More

by Marie Browning

Sterling Publishing Co., Inc.

New York

Prolific Impressions
Production Staff:

Editor: Mickey Baskett
Copy: Sylvia Carroll
Graphics: Dianne Miller, Prepress XPress, Karen Turpin
Styling: Laney Crisp McClure
Photography: Skye Mason, Jerry Mucklow
Administration: Jim Baskett

Every effort has been made to insure that the information presented is accurate. Since we have no control over physical conditions, individual skills, or chosen tools and products, the publisher disclaims any liability for injuries, losses, untoward results, or any other damages which may result from the use of the information in this book. Thoroughly read the instructions for all products used to complete the projects in this book, paying particular attention to all cautions and warnings shown for that product to ensure their proper and safe use.
No part of this book may be reproduced for commercial purposes in any form without permission by the copyright holder. The written instructions and design patterns in this book are intended for the personal use of the reader and may be reproduced for that purpose only.

Library of Congress Cataloging-in-Publication Data Available

10   9   8   7   6   5

First paperback edition published in 2000 by
Sterling Publishing Company, Inc.
387 Park Avenue South, New York, N.Y. 10016
© 1999 by Prolific Impressions, Inc.
Distributed in Canada by Sterling Publishing
℅ Canadian Manda Group, One Atlantic Avenue, Suite 105
Toronto, Ontario, Canada M6K 3E7
Distributed in Great Britain by Chrysalis Books
64 Brewery Road, London N7 9NT, England
Distributed in Australia by Capricorn Link (Australia) Pty. Ltd.
P.O. Box 704, Windsor, NSW 2756 Australia
Printed in China
All rights reserved

Sterling ISBN 0-8069-3935-4 Trade
          0-8069-2267-2 Paper

ABOUT THE AUTHOR
Marie Browning

Marie Browning is a consummate craft designer, making a career of designing products, writing books and articles, plus teaching and demonstrating. You may have already been charmed by her creative designs and not even been aware; as she has designed stencils, stamps, transfers, and a variety of other products for national art & craft supply companies.

You may also have enjoyed books and articles by Marie. She is the author of two other books published by Sterling, *Beautiful Handmade Natural Soaps* (1998) and *Glorious Gifts From Your Garden* (1999). Her articles and designs have appeared in *Handcraft Illustrated, Better Homes & Gardens, Canadian Stamper, Great American Crafts, All American Crafts*, and in numerous project books published by Plaid Enterprises, Inc.

Browning earned a Fine Arts Diploma from Camosun College and attended the University of Victoria. She is a Certified Professional Demonstrator, a professional affiliate of the Canadian Craft and Hobby Association, and a member of the Stencil Artisan's League and the Society of Craft Designers.

Marie Browning lives, gardens, and crafts on Vancouver Island in Canada. She and her husband Scott have three children: Katelyn, Lena, and Jonathan. ∽

Acknowledgments

I would like to thank the following companies for their generous contributions of supplies for creating the projects shown in this book:

Victoria Paper Company, Inc.
80-28 Springfield Boulevard
Hollis Hills, NY, USA
A huge selection of beautiful handmade papers from all over the world, including papyrus, Lokta paper, printed papers, and Japanese papers

Fiskars Inc.
305 S. 84th Avenue
Wausau, WI, USA
Art knifes, hand drill, paper trimmers, cutting mats, rotary cutter, and decorative edge scissors

Boutique Trim, Inc.
21200 Pontiac Trail
South Lyon, MI, USA
Large selection of charms in many finishes including antiqued gold, patina, and copper

American Art Clay Co., Inc.
4717 W. 16th St.
Indianapolis, IN, USA
Polymer Clay, molds, paper casting supplies

Plaid Enterprises
1649 International Blvd.
PO Box 7600
Norcross, Georgia, USA
Acrylic paints, decoupage finish, stencils, and stamps

TABLE OF CONTENTS

BOOKS FOR EVERY PURPOSE, HANDMADE BY YOU

Easy step-by-step construction of books and journals for personal use and gift giving

The word "book" comes from the Old English word *boc* or "written sheet." Throughout history, from the very beginning of mankind, we have ventured to record our ideas and stories. The "written sheet" has been in various forms—from early man's recordings of hunts on a cave wall to Egyptian scribes using hieroglyphs on papyrus rolls or accordion books made from folded bark in Thailand. They all can be considered "books" as they held valuable information about their authors' lives, laws, literature, and culture.

Types of books have varied over time—from clay tablets in ancient Mesopotamia to the folded sheets of paper bound between a protective cover as we know today. It wasn't until Johannes Gutenburg revolutionized printing with the invention of movable type in 1438 that the availability of books became common and available to the masses. We now have a very varied selection of books accessible to us, and the rich history and craft of making bound books is an industry. Books are now made by machines.

Why would you want to create your own hand bound books in this age of mass production? Not only do you get the satisfaction of creating your own book, but you learn the varied skills and techniques that help you craft many unique gifts and greetings for friends and family. You will also enjoy crafting such a useful item to help record your memories, photographs, quotations, and drawings. You can create your own address books, guest books, photo albums or journals. You can construct a book for a gift, changing the paper selection or decoration to suit the recipient, and make it a truly personal gift.

The different book projects presented here follow the history of book styles with folded books and simple bound books for a rich variety of gift presentations. I also present some ideas for creating your own decorative papers and decorative treatments for the book covers. ∞

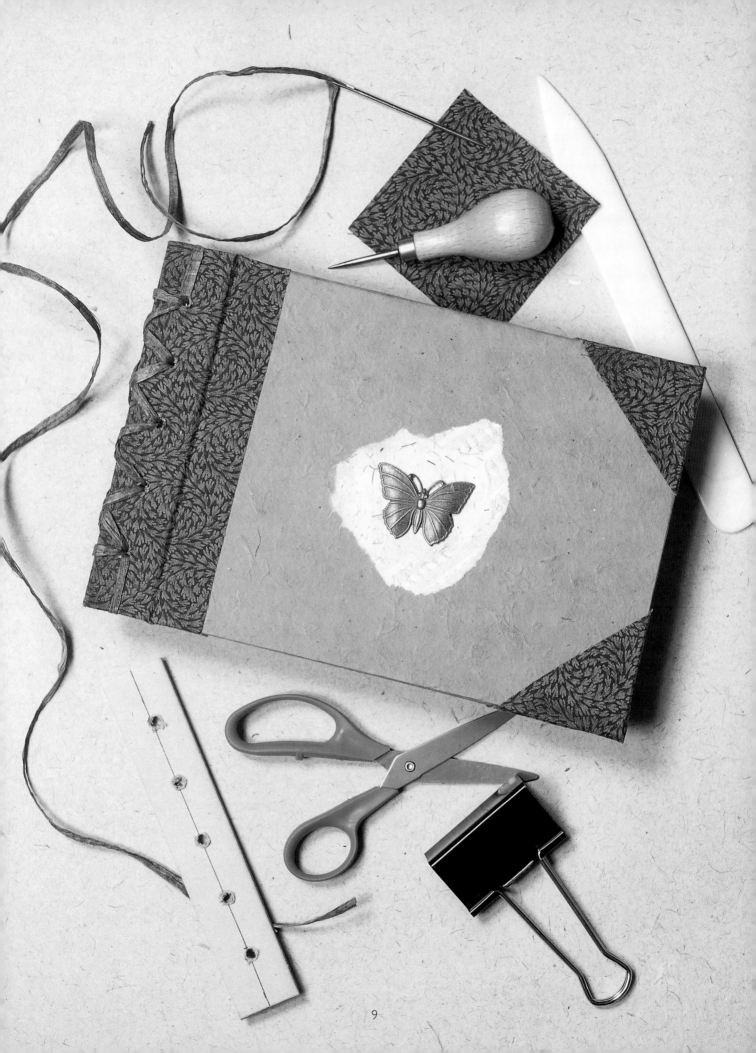

BOOK-MAKING EQUIPMENT

This list of equipment and supplies represents the basic items necessary to create simple hand bound books. More traditional hand bound books require extensive tools such as book presses and sewing frames, but the book projects presented here require simple tools that are easily accessible but essential for successful construction. *The numbers in parenthesis after the items identify that item in the photo.*

BONE FOLDER (1)

This tool is very valuable in the craft of bookbinding. It is formed from bone and is used to fold sharp creases, emboss lines, and to help smooth papers when adhering to a surface. The bone does not bruise the paper when used for folding or pasting as plastic folders tend to do. An eight inch size bone folder with a pointed end is convenient for general work.

RULER (2)

Besides being an essential measuring tool, a straight edge metal ruler with a cork backing is needed for cutting perfectly straight cuts. Wooden and plastic rulers will slide and your knife will cut into them. A selection of lengths from 12" to 24" long are useful in bookbinding projects.

TOOLS FOR CREATING HOLES (3,4,5)

- A **hand drill** (3) with a variety of bit sizes is useful for making holes through the cover and pages for the binding cords. A drill is the easiest for making holes accurately and quickly, but the edges of the holes are ragged and not suitable for some book projects.
- An **awl** (4) is useful for making holes through soft covered spines and handmade paper pages such as the soft covered journals with the corrugated cardboard spines. The awl is also used for marking the placement of the holes through the binding guide.
- **Hand held hole punches** (5) make neat, perfect holes. Both the 1/4" and 1/8" sizes are used. However, they take a long time to punch all the pages for your book. Ask at your local photocopy center, as many provide the service of making holes through stacks of paper for a small fee. You must make sure your directions are clear and the placement of the holes marked clearly so they will be successful in making perfect holes for your pages.
- The **small hole-making tools** that are provided when you purchase eyelets are also very handy for making holes. They can punch through a stack of paper up to 1/4" thick or fabric covered spines, quickly and easily creating perfect, neat holes. You will also require a small hammer to use this tool. Leather crafting outlets also have similar tools of various sizes that can also be used for punching out binding holes.

BINDING GUIDES (PICTURED ON PAGE 20)

Binding guides that you make yourself from scraps of cover boards help you mark holes for binding your book quickly and accurately. They are also useful for marking pages for punching or drilling of holes. If you are making more than one book, you will find the binding guides essential. Use a lightweight card and a 1/8" hand held hole punch to make your binding guides. The sizes of the binding guides are included with each project that requires one.

CLAMPS (6,7,8,13)

Depending on the size of the book, the size and strength of the clamps can vary. A thick rubber band can hold together a small book while a set of strong clamps is needed for larger books. The clamps hold the pages and covers together securely while you make the holes and sew the book together. Large bull clips, plastic clamps, and C-clamps that are used in woodworking are all useful. Clamps that require single hand operation are best. I found a wide selection of clamps at the local hardware store for this purpose. Make sure you guard the surface of the book with scraps of card so the clamps do not mark it.

PASTE BRUSHES (9,10)

Natural bristle brushes in 1" and 1-1/2" sizes are useful for spreading the adhesives when gluing decorative papers to the covers. The large sizes are more efficient than small brushes for applying the adhesives quickly and evenly. Foam brushes can also be used successfully. For thicker adhesives, save small scrap pieces of card to use as applicators for glue.

CUTTING BOARD (NOT PICTURED)

A self-healing cutting mat with a printed grid protects your work surface and provides very accurate cuts. The mat surface seals itself after each cut, so your knife won't follow a previous cut. The mats with 1", 1/2" and 1/4" grid markings make measuring and cutting perfectly square corners a breeze. You must use a cutting mat when using a rotary cutter or the blade will be damaged. Cutting mats range in size from 9" x 12" to mats that will cover an entire table top. Buy the biggest mat your budget will allow.

ADDITIONAL TOOLS (11,12)

- An **ironing board and iron** (11) will be needed for using the fusible adhesives and fabrics. An iron is also useful for flattening papers which have warped or wrinkled. A pressing cloth or a piece of tissue is always used when ironing to protect your surfaces.
- **Pliers** (12) are useful tools for pulling the needle through stubborn holes when binding. ∾

Equipment continued on page 12.

CUTTING TOOLS

Good sharp knives and paper trimmers are used to cut the heavy card for the covers, the paper for pages, and the spine material. Scissors are not able to give you the straight, sharp edges that are essential for successful book crafting. Make sure you have a supply of additional blades for your cutting tools to ensure you'll always have a sharp cutting edge.

- A **scalpel type art knife** (1) or craft knife with a replaceable pointed blade is essential. It is an all-purpose cutting knife for cutting all papers and lighter weight boards.

- a **heavy-duty, hand-friendly knife** with a large blade (2) makes the task of cutting the heavy card for the covers and spines easier. I found one that fits into the palm of your hand with a soft handle that can cut through the heavy board with ease, without your hand getting tired.

- **Rotary cutters** (3) are a must when cutting the fabric spine covers and fabric with fusible adhesives. They can cut through several layers of fabric with ease, creating perfect straight edges.

- **Paper cutters** such as a guillotine paper cutter or a paper trimmer with a sliding blade (4) are useful for cutting pages. You can use your art knife for this purpose, but the larger paper trimmers make the job much easier and faster to accomplish.

- **Sharp craft scissors** (5) are needed for trimming corners, cutting binding cords, and accomplishing decorative treatments such as decoupage. Decorative edged scissors are also useful and fun to use for decorative cover treatments.

- **Decorative scissors** (6,7,8) can create fancy edges for end papers, fly leaves, labels, or other accents that can be added to your book. ∽

"Botanical Journal" – *see instructions on page 102.*

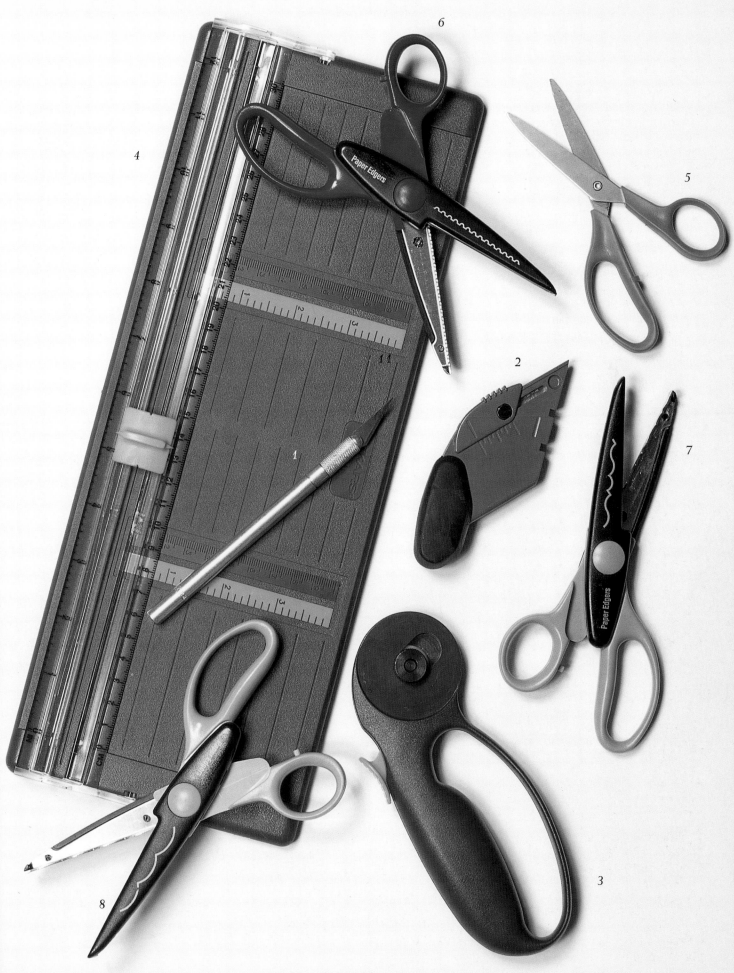

PAPERS

Paper is all around us—made by machine and by hand. It is available in an infinite number of thicknesses, weights, textures, colors, and patterns. You can make your book from papers you purchase or from papers that you have decoratively treated yourself. See the section "Making Decorative Papers" for instructions on making your own unique papers to use for endpapers, flyleaves, or cover coverings.

When planning a scrapbook or photo album to hold precious memorabilia and photographs, look for acid-free or neutral pH balanced papers so it will be preserved for future generations.

Papers are manufactured in standard sizes and weights. Often a paper is identified by the weight of a ream—480 sheets—cut to a given size. Lower weight papers are lighter and thinner. For example, a piece of paper for photocopying is usually a 20 lb. weight paper while a business card could be made of an 80 lb. weight paper.

You will need papers for the following parts of a book:

Inside Pages
Endpapers
Flyleaves
Covering for Covers

∞

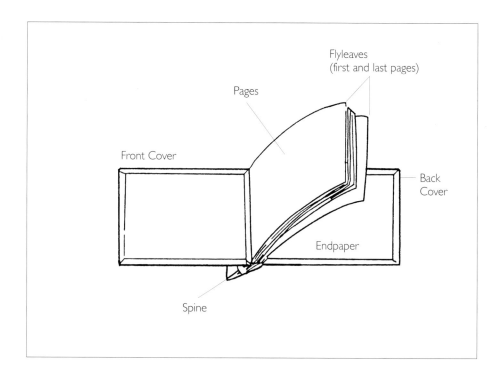

Inside Pages

▦ PAPER TYPES TO USE:

• For journals when only writing and sketching are planned, a 20 lb. paper is an excellent choice.

• The paper available for photocopying is a ready supply of paper that needs only a few cuts to make it the right size for a journal.

• You can also find pads of paper in your local office supply stores that provide ready pages for your book.

• The small sticky note pads are wonderful for making small notepad books.

• Even envelopes can be used for pages for a built-in pocket.

• For the best quality work and a unique look, sheets of handmade papers should be used. Pages constructed out of natural handmade papers such as Lokta from Nepal or Kozoshi from Japan make beautiful pages that are easy to cut and use. ∞

Endpapers & Flyleaves

Endpapers are glued to the insides of the covers to finish the insides of the cover boards. They are usually decorative. They may be of a variety of weights, but should not be too thin or transparent. Historically, endpapers were beautiful and intricate hand marbled papers. Many decorative papers, handmade papers, and papers that you hand decorated can all be used.

Flyleaves are the protective and often decorative pages at the front and back of a book. I choose to use a slightly heavier paper for the flyleaves than what I used for the pages. The front flyleaf is where the book plate is usually located. ∞

Papers & Fabrics For Covering Book Covers

Different weights and thicknesses of paper from thin hand-made Japanese papers to heavy decorated papers can be used to cover the front and back cover boards of your book. Covering with the lighter weight paper is a littler easier than with the thicker, heavy weight papers, as there will be less bulk where you fold over the corners.

Decorative fabrics can also be used for covering your cover boards. Fabric makes for a strong and wear-resistant cover useful for travel journals and diaries. ∾

COVER BOARDS & HINGES

The book boards are the covers that protect the inside pages of your book. The hinges, cut from the same material, enable you to open and close the book. The size of your book will determine the thickness required for your cover board and hinges.

- Mini books (such as the star book or the miniature book) use a lightweight card similar to the thickness of cardboard used for cereal boxes.
- Medium size books and journals, up to about 8" x 10" in size, use a board 1/32" to 1/16" thick. This medium weight board can be matboard (used in picture framing) or illustration board.
- When constructing a larger scrapbook or photo album that requires the strength and stiffness of a heavier board, use display board, fiberboard, or millboard up to 3/16" thick. You can find these boards in fine art supply stores.
- Wooden boards can also be used for the covers of your book. ᕫ

SPINE MATERIALS

The material you use for the spine of the book needs to be strong, flexible, and able to hold up to repeated openings and closings. Traditionally, book cloth such as linen buckram or art linen or leathers were used. However, these materials are difficult to locate and expensive. I have found alternatives for spine construction that are easy to find, inexpensive, and very workable for this purpose.

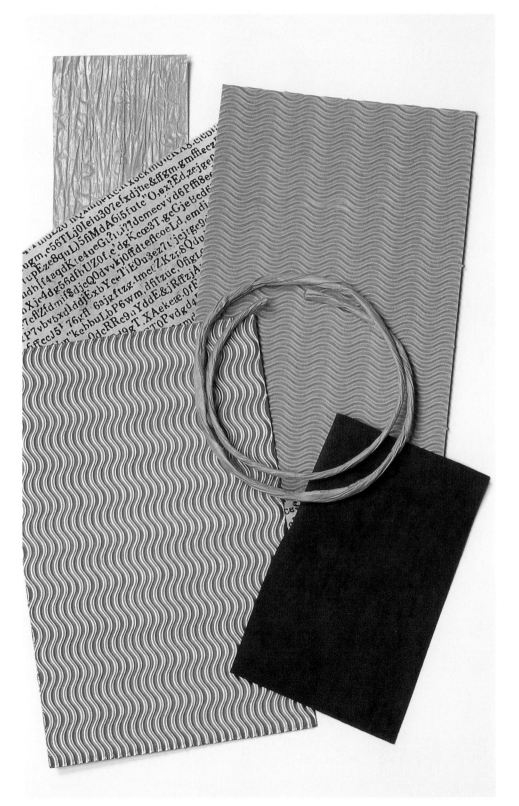

Fabric:

When fabric is used in traditional bookbinding techniques, it reacts badly to the adhesives as the glue seeps through the fabric and damages the surface. But when the fabric is adhered with iron-on fusible adhesive, it becomes a readily available material for all your spine requirements. Heavier, tightly woven cottons and linens, both plain and patterned, and lighter canvas type fabrics are the best for general book construction. You can, however, use decorative fabrics such as velvets, flannels, and muslin. One of the most useful of fabrics is ultra suede, which does not unravel and is available in many colors. Ultra suede is particularly good for making classic, traditional style journals.

Corrugated Cardboard:

Fine corrugated cardboard sheets make wonderful, inexpensive spines for journals and pocket books. It is strong, flexible, and especially good for constructing the simplest books.

Paper:

Paper can be used for your spine material when strengthened by laminating papers to fabric or by laminating papers together. It can also be made stronger with a coat of acrylic varnish or acrylic paint. Making strong, decorative papers for spines is discussed in "Making Decorative Papers." These include faux leather paper and paper ribbon spines. Paper can also be used as an expandable spine when pleated accordion style as in the envelope books. Heavier 80 lb. pastel paper is the best choice for this spine technique. ∾

BINDING MATERIALS

CORDS

Many types of cords or ribbons can be used to bind your book. Thinner widths are easier to thread through the holes, but wider ribbons can also be used for a decorative effect. A selection of both functional and decorative cords include: natural raffia, satin ribbon, sheer ribbon, grosgrain ribbon, velvet cord, leather lacing, jute, waxed linen thread, elastic cord, and garden twine.

BINDING GUIDES

Binding guides that you make yourself from scraps of cover boards help you mark holes for binding your book quickly and accurately. They are also useful for marking pages for punching or drilling of holes. If you are making more than one book, you will find the binding guides essential. Use a lightweight card and a 1/8" hand held hole punch to make your binding guides. The sizes of the binding guides are included with each project that requires one.

NEEDLES

A large eyed tapestry needle is used for pulling the binding cord through the punched or drilled holes. ∾

ADHESIVES

Using the proper adhesives for the different stages of the construction of your book is vital. The glues should be able to hold the heavier papers down but also not seep through the fine papers.

Wallpaper Paste (Methyl Cellulose)
This is a pure adhesive that dries clear. It is archival safe and a good choice for applying papers to the cover boards. I prefer to buy the paste pre-mixed.

All-Purpose Transparent Glue
This is an all-purpose glue that is transparent when applied and will not curl, wrinkle, or discolor the finest of materials regardless of how thin the paper. This glue will also adhere fabrics, leather, or ultra suede. It can be diluted with warm water for a thinner consistency. "YES!" brand glue is my favorite of this type.

Glue Stick
Glue that comes in a stick form for paper has similar qualities to all-purpose transparent glue with the ease of the stick form. Use glue sticks that are non-toxic and acid free for gluing papers down to the cover boards. I generally use a glue stick when constructing smaller book projects.

Decoupage Finish
Acrylic decoupage finish is useful for laminating papers together and for decorative treatments such as the faux leather and decoupage. It can also be used for adhering decorative papers to the cover boards. It goes on smoothly and evenly and dries clear. This glue will seep through the finer handmade papers.

Thick Craft Glue
Use thick, tacky craft glue when a stronger bond is needed such as adhering heavier paper to the cover boards and for gluing on decorative trims and accents like metal charms. When using this glue to adhere papers to the board, apply the glue evenly over the board with a scrap piece of matboard.

Spray Adhesive
Use this to laminate papers together. It is also useful for spraying on the backs of hinge pieces so they do not shift when fusing into the spine material.

Iron-on Fusible Adhesives
These are used to construct your fabric spine by fusing it down and adhering it to the cover boards and hinges. The bond is strong and makes ordinary fabrics into bookbinding tapes by laminating without wrinkles. The edges are fused so there are no worries about the edges of the fabric unraveling or the glue seeping through the fabric. Fusible iron-on adhesive is also useful for laminating fabric to paper and fabric to cover boards. The ultra-hold strength has the best qualities for using in book construction. There is also a fusible adhesive that is sticky on both sides (generally used for applique work) which helps hold everything in place before ironing it down permanently. Always use a pressing cloth to protect your book surface when ironing with any fusible adhesive. ∽

MAKING DECORATIVE PAPERS

Although lovely papers can be purchased for your cover coverings, end-papers, or flyleaves, making your own decorative papers will make your book extra special, and the papers are much less expensive. Papers for bookbinding have been decorated by hand for centuries. We can recreate some of the traditional treatments with simple tools and materials that are readily available. Do not hesitate to combine these techniques for even more varied papers. For example, combine spattering on a stenciled piece, or try salting and the tie-dye method together. The possibilities are endless.

Use These Techniques to Make Your Own Papers

- Combed Paste Paper
- Tie-Dye Paper
- Spattering
- Sponging
- Paper Marbling
- Stenciling
- Salting
- Rubber Stamping
- Using Pressed Flowers & Preserved Leaves
- Decoupage
- Laminated Papers
- Gilding
- Faux Leather

Combed Paste Paper

This ancient method of making designs in colored wet paste on paper is simple and interesting.

To make the paste, mix 1/4 cup of cornstarch with 1/4 cup of cold water until well mixed. This will prevent lumps from forming. Add an additional 1 cup of water to the mix and heat over medium heat until the mixture resembles a thick custard. Keep stirring the mixture while cooking to prevent lumps. You can add up to 1/2 cup more water if the mixture is too thick. Remove the mixture from the stove and mix occasionally while cooling. This paste will not keep long and is best used while fresh. Color the cooled paste with acrylic paint colors, adding small amounts of color at a time. The paste will dry only a shade or two darker.

Here's How:

A shiny coated paper such as kromcote paper or finger-painting paper is used for this decorative treatment. Wet it first by dipping it in and out of a pan of water the size of the paper. (Do not soak the paper, as that will eventually disintegrate it.) Lay the paper out onto a piece of Plexiglas or a flat glass surface and smooth carefully with a damp sponge to get rid of excess water and remove any bubbles.

Apply the colored paste as evenly as you can with a large 2" natural bristled brush. Stroke the color on vertically then horizontally for even coverage. Add pattern and design, using your imagination and a few tools such as cardboard pieces that have notches cut into the side, rubber combs used in decorative paint techniques, fingertips, or sponges. Be careful that your tools do not gouge too deeply into the paper and cause it to tear.

Dry the paper by hanging it on a rack or place it flat on a sheet of freezer paper. The paper will dry with curled edges but will glue down flat when adhered onto a surface. If you wish, you can smooth the paper out with a hot iron (no steam), using a pressing cloth to protect the surface.

Pulled Paste Paper:

Pulled paste paper is produced by painting the colored paste on two sheets of paper which are then laid face to face. Smooth the top paper down gently with your hand, then carefully and slowly pull the papers apart. (If the papers are difficult to pull apart, try using a little less paste on the surfaces.) The papers will have a feathery design and the two sheets will be identical mirror images. ∞

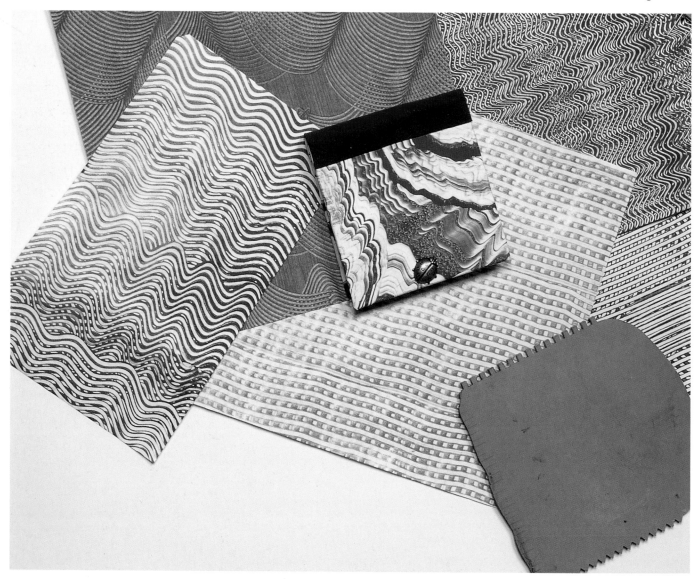

Tie-Dye Paper

I remember doing this technique in kindergarten with paper towels and food coloring. It is actually an ancient Japanese paper treatment called *orizomegami*. The paper should be thin, soft, and absorbent without any added sizes or coatings. Japanese rice paper works best. Use good quality drawing inks that have been diluted with water in a 50/50 mix. Cover your work area with freezer paper and wear plastic gloves.

The rice paper is folded in even accordion pleats, then accordion-folded again in squares, rectangles, or triangles. The folded piece is dipped in clean water, then the corners are dipped into the prepared colors (use tweezers). Start with the lightest colors and work to the darker hues. Squeeze the folded paper under a piece of scrap card on the freezer paper to help the inks spread.

Carefully and slowly unfold the paper and place on freezer paper to dry flat. Flatten the paper with a hot iron when dry. ∞

25

Spattering

Spattering is a paint technique that can make interesting papers quickly and easily, but it can be messy. Use a large piece of freezer paper to protect your work surface. Any type of paper can be used for this decorative painting technique. There are two techniques I like to use; the first method uses a large, stiff brush and the second uses a spattering tool designed for this technique. For both methods, the consistency of the acrylic paint is important, neither too thick nor too thin. I prefer a mixture of one part acrylic paint to one part acrylic extender. Water can also be used to thin the color. You can also use thinned down colored paste (same recipe as the paste paper method) to spatter on your papers.

The **brush method** uses a large, stiff bristled brush. Dip the tip of the brush into the color (not adding too much paint or it will fall on your paper in large blobs). Use a piece of heavy card to stroke over the bristles of the brush to form the spatters. Pull the card towards you or you will end up spattered, too. Add more colored spatters as needed. Let the paint dry before adding a second spattered color, if one is desired.

The **spattering tool** has a stiff bristled end and a moveable wooden handle with a metal bar to move through the bristles to form the spatters. You can control the spatters more easily and it is much quicker than the brush method. Fill the bristles with paint, turn the handle, and watch the specks, dots, and spatters quickly fly onto the paper surface.

Mask the spatters and create interesting patterns on your paper by placing pressed leaves, keys, or any other objects onto your paper surface to mask an area from paint. Let the paint dry, reposition the objects, then spatter with another color. The design

can be built up with this technique to create a rich depth to the paper surface and a uncommonly attractive decorative paper. ∽

Sponging

You can create many soft, fascinating patterns with the sponging technique. The finished surface should not look harsh or show the sponge shape. You want to achieve a piece of paper with a colorful and interesting surface.

All Over Sponging: Use acrylic paint color, a natural sea sponge, and different colors of pastel paper to make this decorative paper. Dampen the sponge with water and squeeze out excess. Pour paint into a disposable plate. Dip the sponge into the paint and work the paint up into the sponge by tapping on a paper towel. You do not want too much paint on your sponge or the pattern will be too harsh. Lightly pounce the sponge on the paper surface to create the decorative surface. Use a variety of colors. There is no need to completely cover the surface, let a bit of the paper color show through for interest.

Sponge Shapes: Try cutting a compressed cellulose sponge into different shapes for sponging a pattern onto your paper. (The sponge will "pop" up to regular sponge thickness when placed in water.) Use acrylic paint for this technique.

Stamping and Block Printing: There are a great many foam blocks and foam stamps available on the market for stamping images. All can be used on paper with fascinating results. Use the recommended paint for the blocks. I prefer water based acrylic paint for all my block printing and sponging designs, for easy cleanup and fast drying. ∽

Paper Marbling

Marbling is floating colors on a thick liquid, then transferring it to a sheet of paper. Traditionally, marbled papers were used for the endpapers of the finest bound books. This craft started as early as the 8th century, and the finest marbled papers were found in Persia and Turkey. It was also used to prevent tampering with what was written on it, like today's security papers. For example, the edges of accounting books were marbled to make the removal of any pages easily seen. The classic marbling technique of floating opaque watercolors (gouache) on a caragheen moss size is complex and demanding. The method presented here is a very simplified technique of floating thinned acrylic paint color on liquid starch.

The liquid starch (size) is used straight from the bottle. Pour it into a low pan slightly bigger than the paper. I use a 10" x 12" disposable foil baking pan for 8" x 10" paper. Absorbent papers such as block printing paper (from fine arts supply stores) or handmade papers are best. Drawing inks or acrylic paints thinned with water work well. The color should spread out on the size without sinking. If it doesn't, add a few drops of Photo-Flo (found at camera shops) to break the surface tension.

Apply the inks or thinned acrylics to the surface with an eyedropper. When the surface is covered with color, use a wooden skewer to swirl the color around to produce your design.

Lay a sheet of the absorbent paper over the size. (Avoid bubbles on the surface or they will become large white spots on your design.) Remove the paper and place on a sheet of Plexiglas. Gently rinse off the excess size over a large bucket or the sink by pouring a cup of clean water over it. Hang the print to dry.

Before making your next print, skim the top of the size with a strip of newsprint to remove any leftover color. ∾

Stenciling

Stenciling designs onto paper or wood is a fast and easy way to decorate. There are hundreds of stencils available in a vast array of motifs. Use a waterbase stencil gel or acrylic paint color to stencil your designs. The most important thing to remember when stenciling on paper with any type of paint is to use very little paint for best results. If your paint is leaking under the stencil, you are using too much! Stencil brushes or dense sponges work best to apply the paint. Load the paint onto your applicator, then remove the excess by tapping on a paper towel. Experiment on a scrap piece of paper before moving to your project. ∽

Salting

This decorative paint technique is used by watercolor artists and silk painters for an interesting design in washed-on color. Use diluted acrylic paint color, watercolor paper, and ordinary salt or coarse salt.

Water down your paint to an ink consistency and brush over the paper. Aim for a washed effect with a variety of shades of the color. While the paint is still damp, sprinkle salt over the surface. Wait until the paint has dried completely before rubbing off the salt and revealing the mottled surface. The salt on the damp paper absorbs the color, leaving a fascinating dappled design in a variety of shades. ∽

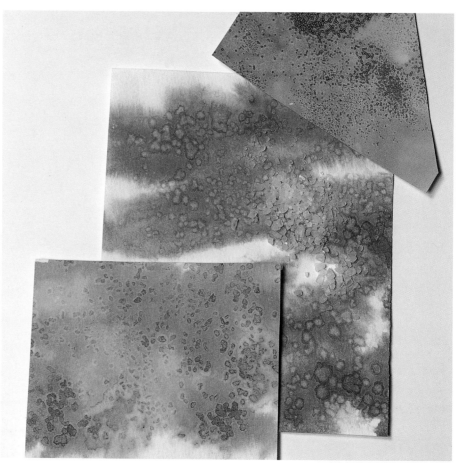

Rubber Stamping

The art of rubber stamping has grown into a beautiful art form with many wonderful techniques. Here are only a few ways you can add images to paper with rubber stamps.

Simple Stamping: The range of motifs available in rubber stamps is huge, from tiny sizes that can be repeated for a design to large sizes for instant coverage. Stamp pads come in a vast array of colors. Most are acid free and safe for memory albums and journals. Make sure your stamp pad has a raised pad so it can be used on any size of stamp. Load the stamp evenly with the ink by lightly tapping it on the ink pad. Press the stamp firmly onto the surface without rocking the stamp. Practice first on a scrap piece of paper.

Thermal Embossing: Embossing is a technique used to raise the stamped image above the surface of the paper. You will need a rubber stamp, a pigment ink pad, embossing powder, and a embossing heat tool (or other heat source such as an iron or toaster oven). There are many embossing powders available—shiny, matte, glitter or iridescent, and many different colors. Stamp the image onto your paper. While the ink is still wet, sprinkle on the embossing powder, completely covering the image. Shake off the excess and place back into the jar. Turn on your embossing heat tool and blow the hot air onto the stamped image for a few seconds. The powder will melt. Do not overheat. If using an iron or a toaster oven, hold the image over the heat source until the powder melts.

(Don't scorch your paper.) The embossing powder melts at a temperature of 350 degrees F., so a hair dryer will not work. When finished, your stamped image will have a raised, dimensional surface.

Layered Embossing: This method layers stamped embossed images and embossing powder to create a pebbly surface. You will need a variety of stamps (simple, small motifs work best), embossing ink pad, colored embossing powder (I used gold and copper), clear embossing powder, an embossing heat tool, and pieces of precut matboard, the color of your choice. Stamp the chosen image on the surface with the clear embossing ink pad. Sprinkle on the gold embossing powder, shake off excess, and heat to melt the powder. Choose a different motif, stamp it on the surface with the clear embossing ink pad, and sprinkle with copper embossing powder. Shake off excess. Heat to melt. Repeat with the gold and copper embossed images to help build up the design. With the clear ink pad, ink the entire surface of the matboard. Tap lightly all over to achieve an even inking. Sprinkle the surface with clear embossing powder, shake off the excess and heat to melt. Your entire surface will be embossed with a clear, pebbled texture. Experiment with different colors of powders, different stamps, and different colored matboard for an endless variety. Use these matboard pieces for your book covers.

Using Pressed Flowers & Preserved Leaves

Pressed flowers and leaves can be used in a number of ways. You can decoupage the delicate flowers to your covers or end papers, as well as laminate them between tissue paper and paper that is used for the end papers, fly leaves or the covering material.

▨ THE PRESSING TECHNIQUE

Pressing plants is a simple method that results in a two-dimensional product suitable for decorative use in bookbinding.

You can use a purchased flower press or use a large book for pressing the flowers and leaves. Pressing plants takes three to four weeks on average.

Harvest the plants in the morning after the dew has dried. Collect flowers in various stages of blooming as well as the leaves and the buds of the plant. Press the plants as soon as possible after harvesting to prevent wilting. Place the plants between two absorbent, smooth paper sheets (I like to use rice paper) in the flower press or heavy book. Do not use paper toweling as it will impart a pattern onto the pressed plants. Different flowers take

The Pressing Technique (cont.)

varied lengths of time to dry. Check the press in about two weeks. You cannot harm the process if you leave the plants in the press after they have dried, but you can damage them if you take them out before the drying process is complete. Store the pressed plants flat in labeled envelopes.

A partial list of flowers suitable for pressing includes: hydrangea, pansy, forget-me-nots, lobelia, ferns, all types of leaves, leaves and flowers of herbs, larkspur, Queen Anne's lace, violets, wild roses, and sweet alyssum.

How to Make Skeleton Leaves

The skeletonizing of leaves is a messy but effective way to bring out the delicate vein structure of the leaves. Pressed and dried skeleton leaves make a beautiful addition to a book bound with natural handmade paper. They can also be used in collage, card designs, and other craft projects. You will be pleased with the small amount of effort it takes to make these unusually dried, lacy pressed leaves.

Materials: Glass saucepan, disposable wooden stick for stirring, *sodium hydroxide (lye), chorine bleach, soft toothbrush, nail brush, 8" glazed ceramic tile, paper towels, and fresh leaves. Some suitable leaves for skeletontizing are: Camilla, rhododendron, ivy, magnolia, beech and holly.
NOTE: Caution must be used when working with the lye as it is very caustic. A splash in your eyes could be dangerous. Read all the directions and cautions on the container before beginning. The nail brush and soft toothbrush should be used for this purpose only; discard after use. Use only glass pots and bowls, as the lye can damage metal and plastic.

Here's How: Place about 12 medium size fresh leaves in the glass saucepan and cover with at least 4 cups water. Carefully pour in 4 tablespoons of lye and mix well. Bring to a slow boil and simmer for about one hour. The liquid will become very dark; this is normal. Take the saucepan from the heat and let cool.

Test a leaf to see if it is ready to proceed. Take the leaf from the lye solution and rinse well in a bowl of clean water. Place the leaf on the tile and gently rub with a soft toothbrush. If the leaf tissue comes away, you are ready to proceed. If the tissue is not coming away from the leaf, place it back into the lye solution and let soak for an extra day. Keep testing the leaf; continue soaking until ready. Different leaves take different lengths of time to become ready in the lye solution. It will depend on how old the leaf is, the potency of the lye solution, and the time of year.
To bleach your leaves, place in a bowl of 2 cups water and 1 cup chorine bleach. You will see them slowly lighten and you can remove them (one leaf at a time) at any time for a variety of shades. Rinse the leaves well in clean water before proceeding.

Place the leaf on the glazed tile, front side down. With the nail brush, gently pounce up and down on the leaf. This action will dislodge the plant tissue, leaving behind the fibrous material or skeleton of the leaf. Do not rub the brush against the fragile leaf as it will tear. Holding the leaf flat on the tile, rinse with a gentle flow of water from the faucet.

Gently remove the leaf from the tile and place on a paper towel. Blot with another paper towel to dry it. Place leaves in a plant press or in a heavy book until completely dry.

Decoupage

Decoupage is a simple decorative paper treatment that is done on the finished front cover of the book. I like to use ripped pieces of decorative papers, fine Japanese papers, and tissue papers left over from other projects. I keep a basket full of scraps just for this purpose. Motifs cut from wrapping paper, paper doilies, pressed flowers, and skeleton leaves can also be decoupaged onto your project.

You will need a 1" sponge brush, decoupage finish, and your chosen paper pieces or cut out motifs. Brush the decoupage finish

onto the backs of the paper motifs, working from the center of each motif out to the edges. Work on a piece of freezer paper to protect your work surface. Arrange the motifs onto your surface and use your fingers to smooth out any wrinkles or air bubbles. Overlap motifs to create interesting compositions. Allow the pieces to dry. If using pressed flowers, coat the book surface with an even coat of finish, then arrange the flowers or leaves on the wet finish. Add an additional coat of decoupage finish to protect your arrangement.

Gilding

Wonderful metallic surfaces can be achieved by gilding with metallic leaf. Metallic leaf comes in gold, silver, and copper. The easiest method of gilding is to spray a piece of matboard with a thin, even coat of spray adhesive. Let the adhesive dry a few minutes until tacky. Now gently lay the fragile leaf onto this sticky surface. Use a dry, soft brush to gently brush the leaf into the adhesive. If there are missed spots, just place another small piece of leaf over the spot and gently tap down with the brush. To remove excess leaf, brush it gently away. Burnish the surface with a smooth, soft cloth.

Dimensional Gilded Motifs: For simple raised metallic images on the gilded board, squeeze out a simple design with a glue gun. Let the glue cool and harden. It will be slightly sticky and the metallic leaf will bond to it. Follow the general gilding instructions to gild the raised glue design.

To protect your gilded surface, brush with a coat of sealer formulated for metallic leaf gilding. Find both the metallic leaf and sealer at fine art supply stores. ∽

Laminated Papers

Freezer paper is handy as a laminating paper. You can laminate fine papers, pressed leaves, or tissue to the freezer paper for a sturdy cover paper. To laminate, place your fine paper on top of the shiny side of the freezer paper. With a hot iron (no steam), press the papers together. The plastic coating of the freezer paper melts, adhering the fine paper to the surface. Pressed flowers can be placed in between to laminate them within the two papers.

Coffee & Tea Staining

You can create interesting stained effects on paper by using a strong tea or coffee solution. Simply dab this solution onto your paper with a sponge brush or drop onto paper with an eye dropper.

Faux Leather

Traditionally, leather was used extensively for bookbinding. It is easy to make your own leather-look-alike papers. Here are three techniques for creating the faux leather look.

Decoupage Method:

With this decoupage method, you can recreate the look of leather very inexpensively. You will need a sheet of pastel paper, a sheet of tissue paper, decoupage finish, and acrylic paint.

Crumple the sheet of tissue paper up tightly. Carefully smooth out the sheet and place it aside. Brush a coat of the decoupage finish on the pastel paper. Work quickly so the finish does not dry out. Place the tissue paper over the wet surface. With your hand, gently smooth down the tissue so it bonds with the pastel paper. The crumpled tissue will create many fine creases and lines that resemble the surface of leather. Let dry. Brush on a top coat of the finish to seal and strengthen the paper. If you choose a tissue color that suits your project, you can use the faux leather paper at this point. If you wish another color, you can paint the faux leather with acrylic paint in the color you wish. This paper is strong enough to use as a spine material in the smaller size journals.

Paper Ribbon:

This paper comes in tight coils and can be untwisted, smoothed out, and used as a very effective spine material. Unravel the paper ribbon and smooth out with a hot iron. Paint the surface with the decoupage finish to strengthen and finish. If desired, antique the paper ribbon with acrylic antiquing medium to bring out the wrinkles. Brush the antiquing onto the paper ribbon, then wipe off excess with a paper towel, leaving the dark paint in the creases and wrinkles. When completely dry, iron the paper ribbon flat. Always use a pressing cloth when ironing on the this paper surface; if the hot iron touches the paper, it will stick and leave a sticky mess on the surface of your iron. You are now ready to iron on fusible adhesive to construct the spine.

Embossed Paper:

To achieve the rich look of beautifully tooled and patterned leather, paint acrylic color onto embossed wallpaper. This wallpaper can be found in large rolls or broader widths at your local paint and wallpaper store. Use this paper as you would any heavy decorated paper to cover boards for book covers. ∾

33

CHAPTER 2

BOOKBINDING TERMS

Accordion Fold: Pages are folded back and forth, somewhat like the bellows on the musical instrument.

Binding: The sewing or lacing the pages to the front and back covers of the book. All the book projects use a simple binding technique in which the binding material is seen and used as a decorative element in the book's composition.

Book Covers: The actual cover of the book which contains the pages.

Deckle Edge: The natural uneven edge of paper that occurs as the wet pulp of the paper flows off the screen when making handmade paper. Deckle edged decorative scissors can also simulate the deckle edge on machine made paper.

Endpapers: The papers adhered to the inside of the book's front and back covers to finish the inside of the cover.

Flyleaves: The protective and often decorative pages at the front and back of a book.

Folio: A folio is formed by folding a sheet of paper in half so that two leaves are produced.

Foot: the bottom edge of a book.

Fore-edge: the unbound edge of the book, it is held to open the book.

Glassine: A transparent, non-stick paper that works well as a guard when rubbing down decoupaged papers, pressed flowers, and cut motifs. You are able to see what you are doing and, if the glue seeps out, the glassine guard will not stick to the surface. I also like to use envelopes made from glassine paper for a transparent container.

Guards: Scrap pieces of matboard are used to guard or protect the surface of the book while clamping. A sheet of freezer paper is also used as a pasting guard to protect your work surface when applying glue to a piece of paper.

Handmade Paper: Paper made by hand using a mold (a screen in a wooden frame) and deckle (flat frame to contain the wet pulp) that is dipped into a vat of water and plant fibers called pulp. The wet fibers form a sheet of paper on the screen. The paper is then couched out (flipped out) onto a couching cloth, then pressed and dried to form paper. Handmade paper has a deckle edge on all sides. Handmade papers, made from a great variety of plant fibers for different papers, are available from all over the world. Rice paper, paper made with long fibers such as silk, straw, mulberry, and other plant fibers, and even papers made from elephant dung are all available for use in bookbinding. Handmade papers come in a variety of weights, but the most used are the text weight which is good for pages and cover weight for covering the book boards.

Hardcover: Hardcover books have very stiff, non-flexible covers to protect the inside pages.

Head: the top edge of the book.

Inside Pages: The actual pages of the book.

Knocking-down: The act of taking all the cut pages of the book and tapping each edge on the table to make the pages even and straight.

Laminate: Fusing or gluing papers together or fabric to paper to create stronger materials or for decorative effects. Adhesives for laminating include fusible iron-on adhesive, spray adhesive, freezer paper, and decoupage finish.

Machine Made Paper: Many beautiful papers are created by machines. We are most familiar with paper made from wood pulp such as newsprint, bond, and cartridge papers. Papers can also be made with cotton fibers, called rag papers, and used for fine drawing, watercolor painting, and printing. Pastel paper and papers with the handmade look are also made by machine. Machine papers are made on a large screen roller. The finished sheets have only two deckle edges.

Marbled Paper: A method of applying a decorative pattern to paper by floating colors on a size. The best marbled papers are made with an opaque watercolor on a caragheen moss size.

Paperbacks: Paperbacks are books with flexible covers.

Rubbing-down: When gluing any papers down to a surface, the bone folder is rubbed across the paper with the flat edge to bond the paper down firmly. Use a piece of scrap paper to protect the paper surface when rubbing-down with the bone folder on delicate or easily marked papers. ∞

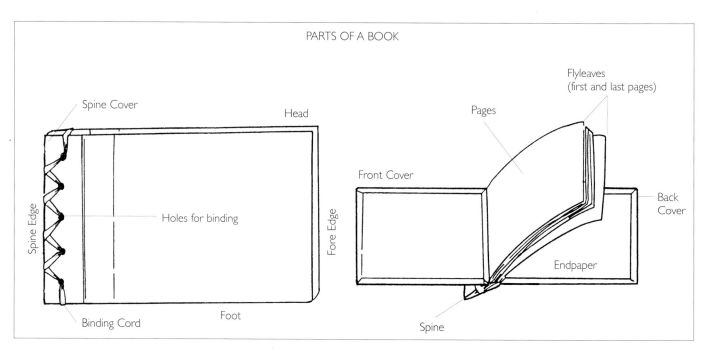

PARTS OF A BOOK

BOOKBINDING TECHNIQUES

To successfully create the projects in this book, you must master the basic techniques. Cutting clean straight lines, folding sharp crisp creases, measuring accurately, and folding paper over corners perfectly are all important skills for making your own books and journals. These skills are easy to master with practice and the proper tools.

CUTTING

Many people cut incorrectly, so these hints for proper cutting will help you master this important skill.

- The key to successful cutting is a good sharp blade. Always have extra blades handy to keep the knife in top cutting form. Remember safety. Keep fingers well back on the ruler to avoid accidents. It is safer to use a sharp blade rather than a dull blade that can easily slip.
- Use the grid markings on your cutting mat for measuring and lining up the paper while cutting. You won't need to make marks on your paper and your corners will be perfectly square.
- When cutting with your metal ruler, hold the ruler down firmly with your non-cutting hand, and keep that hand on the ruler until you've completed the cut. You may need to make several cutting strokes to cut through many layers of paper or heavy card.
- Hold the art knife like a pen, with your index finger (it's your strongest) on top of the handle. You can make cleaner cuts by exerting a downward pressure on the blade while cutting.
- Make sure the blade is held at a constant low angle to the paper, and make strong one-motion cuts towards you. Don't press too hard or you will drag and rip the paper.
- When cutting through heavy cover board do not try to cut it all in one stroke. You will need two or three consistent strokes with a firm pressure to cut through more easily. Use this same technique when cutting through a stack of papers. Do not let up on the pressure while holding the ruler down. Make as many cuts as needed to penetrate all the layers of paper.
- When you have a large stack of paper to cut, it is best to cut it in smaller batches to prevent splaying. With a paper cutter, cut no more than five sheets at a time. With an art knife and cutting board you can do about ten at once.
- Always measure twice and cut once.

FOLDING

Carefully measure and emboss the fold to obtain clean, sharp folds. Use the bone folder and grid on the cutting mat to measure and mark your folds. On each fold, draw the bone folder along the ruler edge towards you, pressing down to emboss a fold line. Fold along this embossed line and use the bone folder to firmly reinforce each fold by smoothing the fold down sharply.

Rather than cutting sheets of paper to size, you can simply fold the sheet into a folio and use in your book with the folded edge at the spine edge. For example, if your book requires pages that are 5-1/2" x 8-1/2", you can fold in half a piece of standard sized (8-1/2" x 11") 20 lb. bond paper.

LAMINATING

With Spray Adhesive:
Spray both pieces of paper and place sticky sides together for a good bond. Rub down with the bone folder for a good connection. Always laminate the papers before cutting them to size to insure that all edges are well bonded.

With Fusible Adhesive:
This method is good for laminating fabric to paper and fabric to cover boards. Peel off the protective sheeting and lay the glue side down onto your fabric. Fuse lightly with an iron to adhere the glue and backing paper to the fabric. Take off the top protective paper and place the fabric with the fusible adhesive glue side down onto the paper or cover board. Use the iron on the highest heat and press the materials together. You can iron too much and the adhesive qualities can be lost. Read the manufacturer's directions for a perfect laminated piece. Always laminate the materials together before cutting to size.

With Freezer Paper:
You can successfully laminate fine papers, such as fine rice papers and tissue papers, to freezer paper for a stronger paper. Place the freezer paper, shiny side up, on the ironing board. Place your fine paper on top. With a hot iron, press the materials together. Turn over and press from the other side. Use a pressing cloth so you do not scorch the fine paper. The fine paper is permanently bonded to the freezer paper. This method, when used with fabrics, only makes a temporary bond that can easily be pulled apart.

GLUING

Use the following helpful hints for successful gluing:
- It is not only important to use the right type of adhesive for a project, it is also important to apply it properly.
- Don't use a lot of glue or it will cause the paper to warp and wrinkle. It can also seep out of the edges and destroy your paper surface. Use a piece of card to "squeegee" out a thin layer of glue when working with a thick adhesive. Use a brush for thinner glues.
- Start applying glue in the center of the paper and work the glue to the outside edges. All the brush strokes should go from the center to the edge to prevent glue buildup at the edges (Fig. 1). Use a piece of freezer paper to guard your work surface when applying the glue.
- Follow the manufacturer's directions carefully when using spray adhesive and iron-on fusible adhesive for premium results. ∞

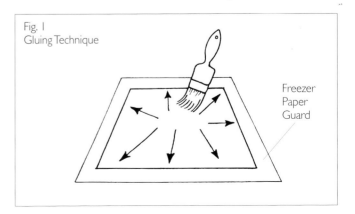

Fig. 1
Gluing Technique

Freezer Paper Guard

CHAPTER 4

BASIC PROCEDURE
FOR MAKING YOUR OWN
JOURNAL, ALBUM, OR BOOK

While different techniques are used for different styles of books, the basic procedure of making covers, spines, endpapers, pages, and other steps are common to all types. The following pages describe the basic procedure to follow.

You will make your
books in this order:

1. Assemble the materials and tools.
2. Cut the papers for cover coverings, spine, inside pages, flyleaves, and endpapers to size.
3. Make the covers.
4. Prepare the spine.
5. Assemble the cover.
6. Attach endpapers.
7. Assemble covers, flyleaves, and inside pages.
8. Drill holes for binding.
9. Bind your book.

ASSEMBLE MATERIALS & TOOLS

Before starting a project, gather all your materials and tools at your work surface. It is frustrating to have to stop your project while you go find something you need for it. The "Equipment" chapter lists all the tools you will need.

Cut Papers to Size

The project section lists the types of materials and sizes for each part of your book. It is helpful to cut all your papers or other materials to their proper size before you begin assembly.

The photo at left shows all the parts of the book assembled to create a basic closed spine book.

Making the Covers

1 Apply a thin layer of adhesive on the wrong side of the decorative covering paper, covering the entire surface. Position the cover board in the center of the paper.

2 Turn cover over and rub-down the paper to the cover with the bone folder edge to bond and prevent wrinkles.

Instructions continue on page 40

MAKING THE COVERS

continued from page 38

3 Run the long edge of the bone folder along the paper down the edges of the cover. This will help crease the edges and prevent any pockets forming along the edge after the paper has been folded over to the inside.

4 Turn the board over to the wrong side. Fold in all the corners at a 45-degree angle and crease lightly (Fig. 1). Trim the corners 1/4" away from the creased line at all corners (Fig. 2).

5 Glue the long sides of the extra paper to the backside of the board, rubbing-down firmly (Fig. 3). Add more adhesive along edges if needed.

6 With the bone folder, press down the corners.

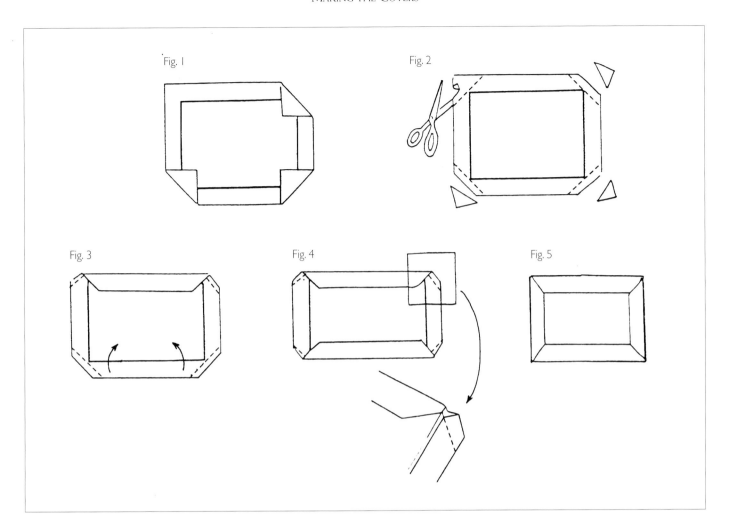

Fig. 1   Fig. 2   Fig. 3   Fig. 4   Fig. 5

7 Before gluing down short sides, fold over a tiny pleat at each corner and rub-down with the bone folder. (Fig. 4 & Fig. 5)

8 Fold over short sides and glue down. Add more adhesive if necessary. This forms perfect bookbinding corners.

MAKING THE COVERS

▥ OPTIONAL FABRIC-COVERED COVERS

Another option to covering your boards is to use fabric. A fabric covering offers a strong, wear-resistant surface for books that will be used everyday such as diaries and journals. The fabric also offers many design possibilities and is readily available. Fabric can be used successfully as a covering material for a cover with the help of iron-on fusible adhesive, rather than glue, which seeps through and shows. This method also works with heavy decorative papers, using the bone folder to fold the paper tightly to cover board edges.

1 Fuse the wrong side of the fabric with the fusible adhesive, following the manufacturer's directions. Cut to the size indicated on the project. Remove the backing paper.

2 Lay the cover board onto the wrong side of the fused fabric, turn to the right side, and lightly press with an iron to hold firmly. Avoid pressing too close to the edges or you could fuse the fabric to the ironing board.

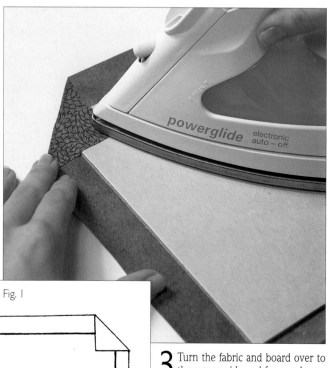

Fig. 1

3 Turn the fabric and board over to the wrong side and fuse each corner up at 45-degrees with the iron (Fig.1). Make sure the fabric is fused tightly up to the corners of the board.

4 Starting with the long sides, and pulling the flaps up tightly against the edges, fuse the long sides to the cover board.

5 Repeat fusing the remaining two flaps up to the cover board. Turn the cover over and fuse again along the edges for a firm bond.

ADDING DECORATIVE FABRIC CORNERS (OPTIONAL)

Adding decorative corners to your book makes a wonderful accent. If you choose to do this, you will need to do this task now before proceeding further. Fabric or thin paper can be used.

It takes only a few steps to make the decorative corners. Cut four 3" squares from the same material that you are using for the spine. Prepare with fusible webbing on backside. Fold in half, then in half again to form four equal triangles. Unfold and lay flat. Trim off two of the triangles 1/2" from the fold (Fig. 1). With the cover closed, fit the corner accent on the lower right hand corner, aligning the fold with the edges of the book. Fuse the corner accent piece in place over the corner. Open the cover, fold the 1/2" overlap to the back, and fuse in place. (Fig.2) Fold over the remaining side of the accent and fuse. Repeat with the remaining corners.

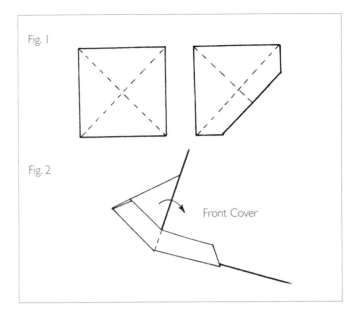

Example of Book with Decorative Corners
Instructions for making this book can be found on page 93.

PREPARING THE SPINE

1. Cut the spine material (fabric, treated paper ribbon, or laminated paper) 2" larger than the dimensions of the finished spine piece indicated in the project instructions. Cut a piece of fusible adhesive slightly smaller than the spine material.
2. Fuse the adhesive to the wrong side of the spine material, following the manufacturer's directions. Let cool, leaving the backing paper in place.
3. On the cutting mat, cut the fused spine material to the cover size given in project instructions, using the rotary cutter. This will ensure good adhesion to the cut edges of the spine material.
4. Fold the spine in half lengthwise and crease firmly. This will mark the center of the spine and help you align the hinges and covers.
5. Remove the backing paper. The spine is now ready to fuse to the covers and hinges to construct the cover for your book.

ASSEMBLING THE "OPEN SPINE" COVER

This method uses two spine pieces that are adhered to both the front and back cover, leaving the spine edge of the book open. After the cover boards have been covered with the decorative papers or fabric and the spine has been constructed, you are ready to put the covers, hinges, and spines together to form the cover of the book.

1 Place one of the prepared spine pieces on the ironing board, wrong side up. Line up the hinge piece below the fold in the middle of the spine material (Fig.1). Place the cover board directly below the hinge piece, with 1/4" between the two. (Fig.2).

2 Cut off the excess spine material corners in a curve, leaving 1/4" between the corner of the board and the cut (Fig.3).

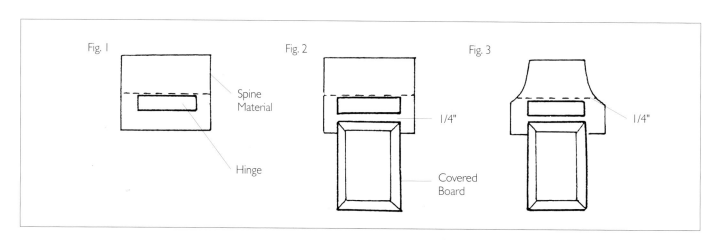

Fig. 1

Spine Material

Hinge

Fig. 2

1/4"

Covered Board

Fig. 3

1/4"

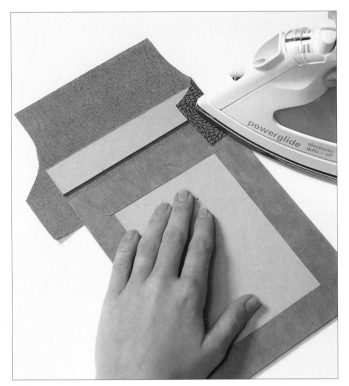

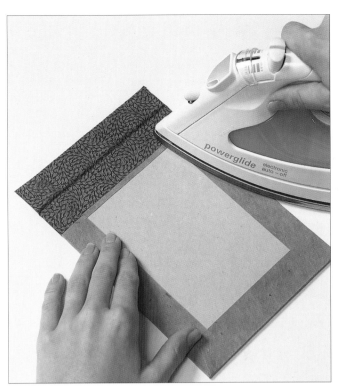

3 Fold the side flaps of spine down onto the board and hinge and fuse to hold. With the tip of the iron, press down the corners so they are snug against the corner of hinge. (Fig. 4). Repeat with the other side flap.

4 Fold the top piece down and fuse to the board making sure the spine material is tight up against the board edge, with no pockets. With the tip of the iron, fuse between where the hinge meets the board (Fig.5). Repeat with the other cover, hinge, and spine piece.

The completed hinged covers are now ready to have the endpapers glued onto the insides, the cut pages inserted, and holes made for the binding.

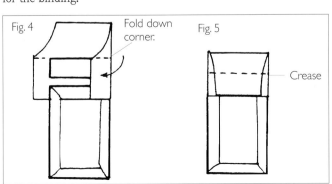

Example of "open spine" cover.

ASSEMBLING THE "CLOSED SPINE" COVER

This method uses a single spine piece and the spine material covers the spine edge of the book. After the cover boards have been covered with the decorative papers or fabric and the spine has been constructed, you are ready to put the covers, hinges, and spine together to form the cover of the book.

1 Place the prepared spine wrong side up on the ironing board. Position the hinges and front and back covers on the spine as shown in Fig. 1. You may want to spray the backs of the hinge pieces with spray adhesive to help hold them in place while constructing the covers.

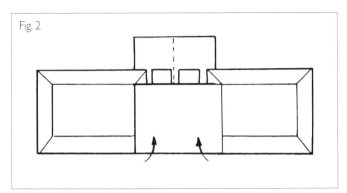

Fig. 2

2 Fold up the bottom part of the spine and fuse with the iron to hold.

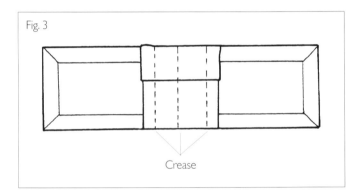

Fig. 3

Crease

3 Fold down the top part of the spine and fuse (Fig. 2). Turn over and iron down the front of the spine. Use the tip of the iron and fuse between the covers and hinges on both the front and the back (Fig.3).

The cover is now ready to have the endpapers glued onto the insides of the front and back covers, the pages inserted, and holes made for the binding.

Fig. 1

Wrong Side
Spine Cover

fold down

2"

Front Cover
(wrong side up)

Back Cover
(wrong side up)

1/4"   1/2"   1/4"

fold up

Crease to mark center.

ATTACHING ENDPAPERS

After the spine has been attached to the cover and hinges, you are now ready to glue in the end papers. Endpapers are adhered to the insides of front and back covers. These hide the turned-in edges of the book covering and finish off the insides of the covers. They are often decorative as well as functional. Endpapers are cut 1/4" smaller than the book covers and are glued or fused in place with a slight margin around them on the fore edges and top and bottom edges of the book. Press them down smoothly with the bone folder.

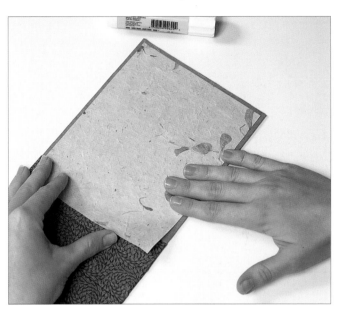

ASSEMBLING FLYLEAVES AND INSIDE PAGES

After the spine has been attached to the cover and hinges, and the endpapers are glued in, you are ready to assemble the inside pages and flyleaves. The flyleaves are placed at the beginning and end of the inside pages. First, knock down (tap down) each edge of the stack of papers to make all the edges even and straight. Place the stack of papers into the prepared spine and covers, aligning the fore edge of the pages to the fore edge of the endpapers. Clamp to hold all in place securely.

DRILLING HOLES FOR BINDING

There are two techniques for drilling holes for binding the pages and covers together. Use either Technique #1 or Technique #2 for drilling your pages.

▓ TECHNIQUE #1
Using a Drill to Make Your Holes

1 Use the binding guide indicated for the project and place it even atop top, bottom and edge of spine. Mark for hole placement. You can use an awl to mark the placement of the holes or light pencil marks.

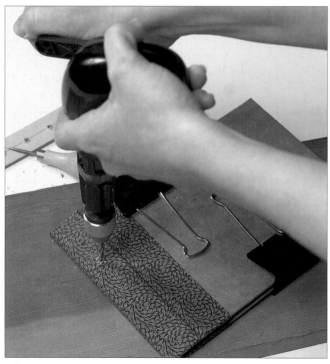

2 Place the book over a piece of scrap wood that can be drilled through. Drill where marked. Drill through the covers and pages right through to the other side. A 1/8" to 1/4" size bit works well for holes through which most binding cords will fit.

3 Leaving the clamps in place, remove any bits from the drilling with the sticky side of the tape to clean up before binding.

TECHNIQUE #2

Using an awl to Make Your Holes

1 Carefully mark the holes, using the binding guide, so the book will be properly aligned. Place the book over a piece of scrap wood and punch carefully where marked using firm pressure on the awl.

TECHNIQUE #3

Using a Hole Punch to Make Holes

1 Punch holes with the punch. Don't try to punch too many pages at once or the holes will become misaligned and messy. You will need to mark each stack of pages you punch carefully with the binding guide.

2 Metal eyelets can be added to the cover holes for a decorative touch and to reinforce them.

BINDING

The binding cord holds your book together and is the final step of the book's construction before decorative cover treatments.

▓ BINDING TIPS

- It is important that your binding cord is strong and that the holes are large enough for the cord to go through as many as three times.
- The binding cord should be cut three times the length of the spine plus 12". The measurement will be indicated in the project instructions.
- Use a pair of pliers to pull the needle through the holes if you find it hard to pull through by hand.
- Another helpful way to pull thick cords or ribbons through the binding holes is to pull the binding cord through with a loop of strong thread that has been pulled through the holes as shown in Fig. 1. This works well for thick decorative cords that you are unable to thread through a needle.
- Two binding techniques are offered here. Practice lacing on your binding guide before binding your book. Feel free to experiment and create your own laced designs.

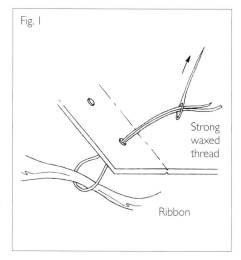

Fig. I

Strong waxed thread

Ribbon

Square Binding

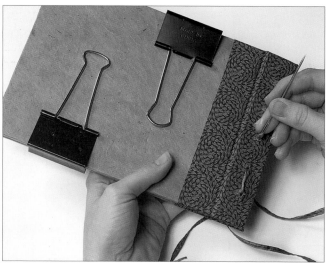

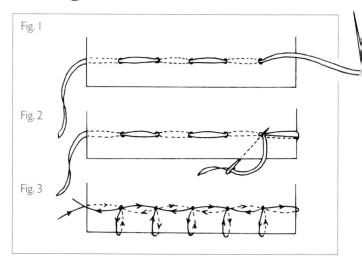

Fig. 1

Fig. 2

Fig. 3

1 Thread the binding cord or ribbon through a large-eyed needle.

2 Insert needle into first hole at head of book. Weave down the spine with a simple running stitch (Fig.1). Leave a 6" tail at the head of the spine.

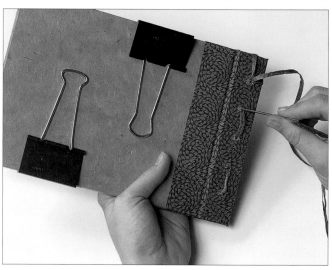

3 At the foot of the book, bring the cord or ribbon up and around the foot and through the last hole. Make a stitch at right angles to the running stitch and bring down through the same hole (Fig.2). Stitch over to the next hole.

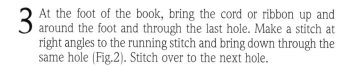
4 Repeat the same right angle stitch up the spine to the head of the book. The ribbon goes through each hole three times. You may need to use pliers to help pull the needle through.

5 At the head, tie a double knot in the back close to the top hole. Trim ends. Add an extra drop of white glue on the knot for extra hold. Let dry.

V Binding

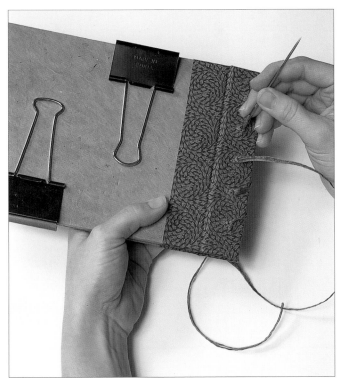

1 Thread the binding cord through a large-eyed needle.

2 Come up from the back through the first hole. Leave a 6" tail at the head of the spine.

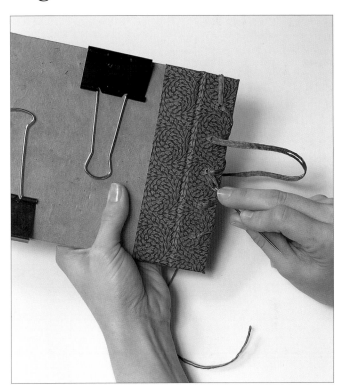

4 Make the last stitch at the foot of the spine and come around to the same hole.

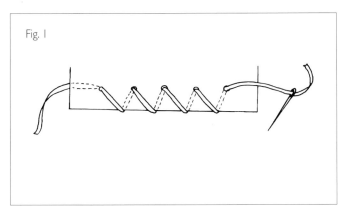

Fig. 1

3 Take the binding cord around to the back and up through the second hole (Fig.1). Continue down the spine with the same diagonal stitch.

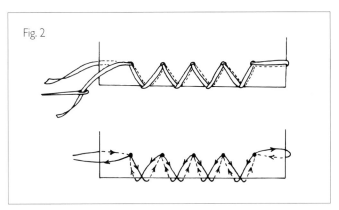

Fig. 2

5 Make the same stitches back up to the head of the spine (Fig. 2).

6 Make a double knot at the back close to the top hole. Trim ends. Add a drop of white glue on the knot for extra hold. Let dry.

ACCENTS FOR YOUR BOOKS

You can further accent your handmade books and journals with metal charms, ribbons, lace, buttons, shells, and a host of other embellishments. The projects show just a few ideas for extra accenting. When adhering heavy objects such as the charms, use a thick, tacky craft glue for best results

METAL CHARMS

Even though you can buy antiqued charms, they can also be easily painted the color of your choice and antiqued to look like an aged enameled piece. I find the charms too brassy for some projects. This painting technique can soften the look and make it match the book you are accenting.

Using acrylic paint and a stencil brush, stipple the color onto the charm. Let it dry a few minutes then wipe the paint from the surface with a soft cloth. The paint will stay in the creases of the design, highlighting the details. You can also carefully paint the different parts of the charm with colors before wiping off the excess.

SEALS AND EMBELLISHMENTS

You can easily create beautiful seals and embellishments with polymer clay and rubber stamps. Roll a small amount of the clay into a small ball. Flatten out slightly. Push a rubber stamp into the clay to create a decorative impression. Follow the manufacturer's directions for baking the clay in your home oven. These clay embellisments look great when rubbed with some metallic wax.

For larger embellishments, roll out a small, thin sheet of polymer clay before impressing your stamp into the soft clay. After the clay is baked, it can be sanded, sealed with a water base varnish, and painted to bring out the details. The same method for antiquing metal charms works on the polymer clay seals and embellishments.

BOOK MARKS

Leftover materials are great to use for making books marks. Use a hole punch to make a hole at the bottom center of the bookmark. Use an eyelet to reinforce the hole, then add a decorative tassel, ribbon, or cord.

LABELS

I like to use labels as bookplates for the flyleaves of my books. Labels can also be used on covers. You can find labels in copy-right-free clip-art books or you can make your own labels by stamping a rubber stamp motif onto a piece of parchment and glu-ing it to the flyleaf. You can also find colorful, decorative labels in book stores.

The purpose of adding the labels is to have a nicely bordered area for writing in messages, such as the name of the book, or the name of the book's owner, date, etc.

Use these designs and your copier to create your
own labels for bookplates or covers.

BOOK
PROJECTS

Now that you have learned all the basic book making techniques, it won't be hard for you to create marvelous books to use yourself or give as gifts. In the chapters that follow, specific materials lists and instructions are given for a variety of books that I have created. Please feel free to use your own creativity to choose papers you love and embellishments that will make your book special. There are 60 books shown so I am sure you can find several you would like to re-create.

In the following chapters
you will learn how
to make:

Accordion Books
Folded Books
Open & Closed Spine Journals
Albums with Wood Covers
Fabric-Covered Books
Envelope Books
Miniature Books
and
A Surprise Star Ornament Book

CHAPTER 5

FOLDED BOOKS

Folded books of all kinds are fun to make and great to give as unique gifts. Accordion style books are the easiest books to make and require only simple cutting, folding, and gluing skills to complete. The accordion method of bookbinding was used in ancient China and in southeast Asia where they were created from silk and folded bark. The projects include some variations to the accordion book for a wonderful variety for gift giving.

Shown in this photo are some of the paper parts assembled to create some of the folded books you will find in this chapter.

BASIC ACCORDION BOOK

The finished accordion books are fun to display when finished with an inspirational or humorous saying inside. To hold the book together I like to use elastic cord for a simple, decorative closure.

The following page gives instructions for making the basic accordion book. The photo below shows the book open.

BASIC ACCORDION BOOK

Finished Book Size: 3-1/4" x 4-1/4"

MATERIALS:

When constructing these books, a medium weight board, about 1/32" thick, works well for the covers. The pages should be constructed with pastel paper. The pages are cut slightly smaller than the covers to prevent them being damaged.

Book Part	Construction Material	# to Cut	Cutting size
Front and back covers	Medium weight board	2	3-1/4" x 4-1/4"
Coverings	Decorative paper	2	5-1/4" x 6-1/4"
Pages	Pastel paper	1	4" x 24"
Binding cord	Metallic elastic cord	1	10"

HERE'S HOW:

1. Cover the front and back cover boards with the decorative paper.
2. Carefully mark the pastel paper every 3", score, and accordion-fold to construct the pages. You should have eight pages. The number of folded pages is always an even number, so if you would like to increase the number of pages to ten, you will need to add an extra 6". Many pastel papers are not long enough to make extra pages so the best solution is to glue the long pieces together to form longer books.
3. Glue the front page to the back of the covered board. Rub-down with the bone folder to bond. Repeat with the back page onto the back covered board.
4. Use two large bull clips to clamp the book together while drying.
5. When the glue has dried, embellish the front cover with added accents. Tie the two ends of the elastic cord together and slip over two opposite corners to hold your finished book together. ∽

BOOKS SHOWN IN THE PHOTO

Seaside Theme

This accordion book was covered with Japanese Suminagashi decorative paper (a form of marbled paper) and decoupaged with torn pieces of natural handmade paper and gold tissue paper. Accents on the front cover include small seashells, sea theme gold charms, and natural jute string. Silver elastic cord holds the book together.

Garden Theme

This accordion book was covered with handmade paper using a combed purple paste technique. Then the paper was decoupaged with pieces of torn wrapping paper and gold tissue paper. A gold bee charm accents the cover. Gold elastic cord was used to hold the book together.

Fancy Page Accordion Books

The pages of this accordion book style have been decoratively cut to form fancy pages, giving a wonderful surprise when opened. The basic sizes and techniques of the Basic Accordion Book were used, but the page designs were cut with a sharp art knife before gluing onto the cover boards. Many charming styles can be developed using the cut paper doll method as was used in the teddy bear accordion book shown. For best results, keep the designs simple and the cutting to a minimum. Words can be created by cutting out letters from the pages as well. Be creative and mix the cut motifs with letters to create an exciting greeting.

The teddy bear motif, a variety of other motifs, and a complete alphabet are provided as patterns on the following pages, so that you can try cutting some Fancy Page Accordion Books.

Books Shown in the Photo

Sunny Day Cheer

Book covers are covered with natural and gold striped paper, then decorated on front with white and gold tissue paper and a sun stamped-and-gilded motif. Inside pages are natural color pastel paper cut to spell "CHEER." One "E" has a dangling star. Gold elastic cord is placed over the corners to hold the book closed.

Teddy Bear

Book covers are done in the faux leather finish. The front is decorated with torn bits of gold tissue paper, red/gold plaid tissue paper, and a brass teddy bear charm. Inside pages of natural pastel paper are cut into the shapes of teddy bears

PATTERN FOR FANCY ACCORDION BOOK
Alphabet

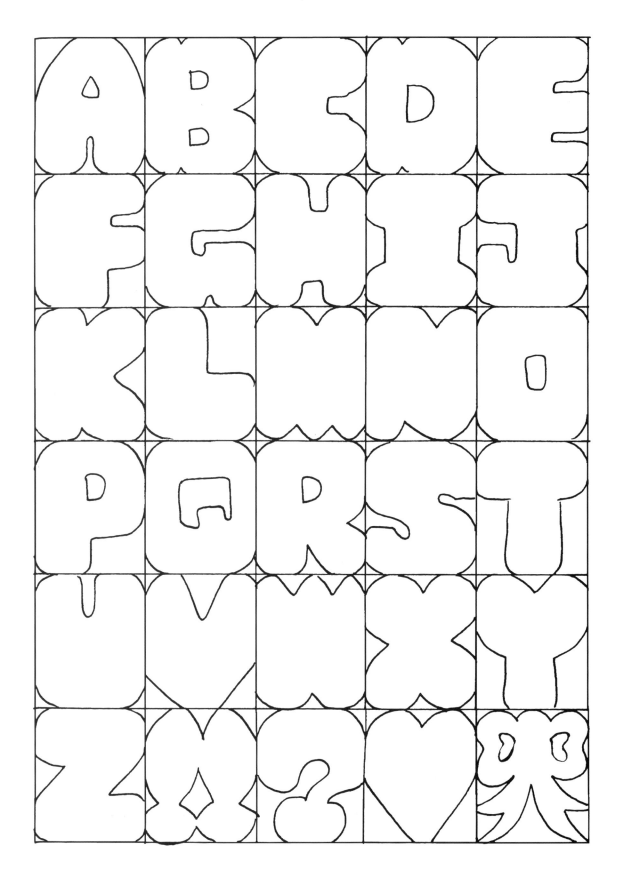

PATTERNS FOR FANCY ACCORDION BOOK

Teddy Bear

Funky Star

Tree

Butterfly

ACCORDION REMINDER BOOKS

An anniversary or birthday book can be created with the accordion style to make a lovely reminder for all the anniversaries, birthdays, and other important days of family and friends.

Finished size: 3-1/2" x 6-1/2"

MATERIALS:

Book Part	Construction Material	# to Cut	Cutting size
Front and back covers	Medium weight board	2	3-1/2" x 6-1/2"
Coverings	Decorative paper	2	5-1/2" x 8-1/2"
Pages	Pastel paper	1	6" x 24"
Binding cord	Metallic elastic cord	1	15"

HERE'S HOW:

1. Follow the directions for the basic accordion book for the construction.
2. You should have eight pages. Write the twelve months of the year on the front and back of the six inside pages. Write in family and friends birthdays and anniversaries in the corresponding month and you will never again miss a celebration. ∞

BOOKS SHOWN IN THE PHOTO

Birthday Book

The birthday book is covered with a gold and silver grid patterned rag/wheat text paper, and the pages cut from tan colored pastel paper. The binding that holds the book together is a 24" length of sheer ribbon glued to the center of the back cover before the pages were glued in. The front of the birthday book is accented by a piece of paper framed with a gold frame charm.

Dragonfly Book

The dragonfly accordion book was covered in green and gold checked wrapping paper and pages were cut from green pastel paper. The front cover was adorned with a piece of torn green paper and a gold dragonfly charm. The book is held together with a gold elastic cord.

POCKET ACCORDION BOOKS

The instructions for the Pocket Accordion Book are the same as the Basic Accordion Book with a few added steps when folding the pages. Use the basic book dimensions or the dimensions for the birthday book if you wish a larger pocket accordion book. The only difference in the construction of the pocket style book is that the pages are folded up to hold small objects such as stamps, business cards, recipe cards, or stickers. When you calculate the size of paper for the book, cut the page piece as long as the height of the book plus an extra few inches for the pocket. This extra piece is folded up, and then the accordion folds are made to create the pages complete with pockets.

BOOKS SHOWN IN THE PHOTO

Business Card Book

The monogrammed business card pocket book is covered with a decorative gold filigree paper and accented with gold charms that are antiqued with cream colored acrylic paint. The fancy monogram is added with a gold paint pen. The pages are made from a soft brown pastel paper, and a piece of gold elastic cord holds the book together. The front and back cover boards are 3-1/4" x 5". The pastel paper is cut to 8" x 24" with a 3-1/4" folded pocket.

Stamp Book

The small stamp pocket book is covered with a handmade Lokta and Ketuki fiber paper from Nepal. The pages are cut from a translucent parchment paper and are slotted and sewn to hold stamps. The cover is decorated with postage stamps and a rubber stamped title embossed with gold. The waxed linen thread is for decorative purposes only and is threaded through small holes reinforced with tiny silver eyelets. The front and back covers measure 2-3/4" x 2-3/4". The parchment paper for the pages measures 14" x 4" with a 1-1/4" folded pocket. The pages are measured and folded every 3-1/2". The style of this pocket book has pages larger than the covers for a decorative effect.

PHOTO ACCORDION BOOK

The photo accordion book was designed with a picture window in the front and uses heavy card for the cover boards to protect the pages of precious photographs.

Finished size: 4" x 5"

MATERIALS:

Book Part	Construction Material	# to Cut	Cutting size
Front and back covers	Heavy weight board	2	4" x 5"
Coverings	Dark blue pastel paper	2	6" x 7"
Pages	Dark gray pastel paper	1	4-3/4" x 22-1/2"
Binding cord	Silver elastic cord	2	12"

HERE'S HOW:

The directions are the same as the Basic Accordion Book with the following changes:

1. From the front cover board, cut a 2-1/2" x 3-1/2" window.
2. When covering the front cover with the window, cover the outside edges first. Cut through the window from corner to corner to cut an X in the covering. Fold over the inside flaps and glue to the back.
3. For the pages, mark every 3-3/4" to form six pages.
4. Before gluing the first page to the back of the front cover, place in a photograph and a piece of translucent parchment paper to show at the front. The photographs are placed in the book with silver photo corners and the journaling is done with a silver paint pen. ∽

WANDERING BOOKS

The Wandering Accordion Books are pure fun! They unfold to create a three dimensional display of the contents that makes them an extraordinary greeting for friends and family. The covers are constructed the same as the Basic Accordion Book, but the pages are cut very differently.

Finished size: 3-1/4" x 4"

MATERIALS:

Book Part	Construction Material	# to Cut	Cutting size
Front and back covers	Medium weight board	2	3-1/4" x 4"
Coverings	Decorative paper	2	5-1/2" x 6-1/2"
Pages	Pastel paper	1	9" x 15"
Binding cord	Metallic elastic cord	1	10"

HERE'S HOW:

1. Cover the front and back covers with decorative paper.
2. Divide the page piece as indicated in Fig. 1 by marking and scoring the lines with the bone folder. Cut away the waste paper indicated.
3. Starting with the top left corner, accordion-fold the pages, rubbing down the folds with the bone folder.
4. Glue the pages into the covers and clamp to hold while drying. I find it easier to add my sentiments or wording after the book has been constructed. ∞

BOOKS SHOWN IN THE PHOTO

Overcoat Wandering Book

This is a cute "Get well" greeting. It reminds the recipient to "Button up your overcoat..." The cover boards are covered with blue checkered paper. The pages are cut from royal blue pastel paper. The overcoat is constructed from brown tissue paper laminated to brown pastel paper. A large blue button decorates the front to finish the overcoat.

Angel Wandering Book

"Wherever you may wander; your guardian angel will be with you." This lovely little book is covered with handmade salted paper and decoupaged with silver and white paper scraps. The pages are cut from white pastel paper, and a little angel charms the front cover.

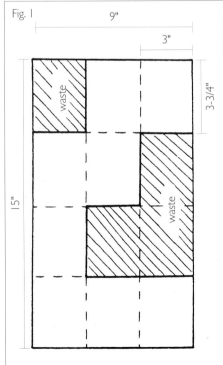

Fig. 1

Triangle Accordion Books

The Triangle Accordion Book is a variation of the Basic Accordion Book. The general construction varies in the covering of the sharp corners and the folding of the pages.

Finished size: 3" x 6"

Materials:

Book Part	Construction Material	# to Cut	Cutting size
Front and back covers	Medium weight board	1	4" x 4"
Coverings	Decorative paper	1	6" x 6"
Pages (8 pages)	Pastel paper	1	3-3/4" x 15"
(or 12 pages)	Pastel paper	1	3-3/4" x 22-1/2"
Binding cord	Metallic elastic cord	1	10"

Here's How:

1. Cut the 4" square of matboard in half, corner to corner, to construct the front and back triangular cover boards.
2. Cut the decorative paper in half, corner to corner.
3. Cover the cover boards. Take special care when folding the sharper corners on the triangular cover boards.
4. Mark off the page piece in 3-3/4" sections. Emboss the lines with the bone folder. You should have four sections marked off. Score a fold, corner to corner, in each section. You now will have eight triangular pages to carefully fold up accordion style. The paper size is also given to make a book with twelve pages.
5. Glue the first page to the inside of the front cover and the last page to the inside back cover. Clamp to hold while drying.
6. Use the elastic cord with a twist in the middle at the back between the two bottom corners to hold your book together. ∞

Books Shown in the Photo

Bee Triangle Book

This book uses handmade paper created with the combed paste technique as the covering for the covers and white pastel paper for the pages. The front is adorned with a honeycomb shaped piece of gold tissue and a gold bee charm.

Sea Theme Triangle Book

This book is covered with homemade salted paper and scraps of handmade paper. The pages are cut from a decorative printed paper. The front is accented with sea theme charms that have been antiqued with green acrylic paint and with a saying written with a green felt pen.

Sky Triangle Book

The sky book is covered with hand sponged and spattered paper. The pages are cut from a bright blue pastel paper. Gold charms accent the front, and a piece of metallic sheer ribbon holds the book together.

DOUBLE ACCORDION BOOKS

The Double Accordion Book takes more time to construct, but is dramatic when opened up and displayed on a table or mantel.

Finished size: 3-1/4" x 5"

MATERIALS:

Book Part	Construction Material	# to Cut	Cutting size
Front and back covers	Medium weight board	2	3-1/4" x 5"
Coverings	Decorative paper	2	5" x 7"
Pages (main piece)	Pastel paper	1	4-3/4" x 24"
Pages (inside piece)	Pastel paper	1	4-3/4" x 18"
Binding cord	Metallic elastic cord	1	10"

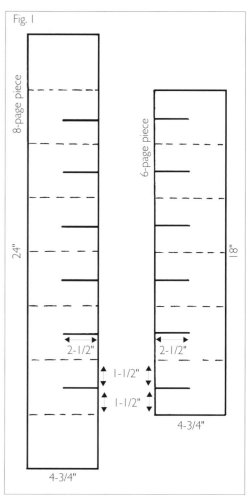

Fig. 1

8-page piece — 24" — 4-3/4"

6-page piece — 18" — 4-3/4"

2-1/2"   2-1/2"

1-1/2"

1-1/2"

HERE'S HOW:

1. Cover the cover boards with the decorative paper.
2. Prepare the pages by marking off and scoring the pages every three inches. One page piece will have eight pages and the other will have six pages.
3. Following Fig. 1, cut slits in the 8-page piece on the inner six pages, leaving the first and last pages uncut. Follow the diagram and cut slits in the 6-page piece as indicated. Accordion-fold each page piece.
4. Glue the 8-page piece into the book covers and clamp to hold until dry. When dry, carefully align the cut slits of the 6-page piece with the inner slits on the 8-page piece and work together with care.
5. To write in your double accordion book, lightly pencil the words for positioning while the book is fully constructed then take the pages apart. Lay both pages out flat and write your words in permanently. When finished, reconstruct the pages. ∞

BOOK SHOWN IN THE PHOTO

The cover boards are covered with hazelnut colored Jerusalem Java natural paper. The pages are cut from mushroom colored pastel paper. The front is adorned with scraps of black paper and a handmade polymer clay piece to look like a fragmented piece of ancient Egyptian tablet. Make your own by flattening a small piece of gold polymer clay and smoothing down the surface. Push a rubber stamp with Egyptian hieroglyphs into the flattened piece to etch in the design. Bake the piece according to the package directions. When cooled, antique the piece with black and red acrylic paints.

CHINESE FOLDED SCROLL

The Chinese pasted sheets of paper and silk together, then folded the long strips into accordion style scrolls. Scented wood covered with silk brocade was used as covers to protect the scroll. This project was inspired by the ingenuity and calming philosophy of the Chinese with the scroll containing inspirational words to make a perfect blessing for a newlywed couple.

Finished size: 2-1/4" x 10"

HERE'S HOW:

1. The book shown in the photo uses a decorative paper from India with a gold lattice printed on burgundy. Cover the front and back cover boards with decorative paper.
2. Score the page piece every 2" and fold accordion style. You will have six pages.
3. Glue the first page to the inside of the front cover and the last page to the inside of the back cover. Clamp to hold while it dries.
4. Decorate the page inserts with inspirational words such as "Joy" and "Peace" with a brush and black ink. When dry, glue to the folded pages. One of the pages does not have an insert. This gives you an area on which to write a personal message to the recipient with a gold paint pen. A Chinese chop is used to sign the work on the last page.
5. Front cover decorations include: Decoupaged scraps of burgundy paper; a stamp; a piece of tan paper decorated with a Chinese characters rubber stamp that has been thermal embossed with black powder; a gold fan charm; and a seal made from polymer clay.
6. Make the closure by threading the bead with both ends of the gold cord. Knot the ends of the cord together. Place the cord loop around the book and slide the bead up to hold the book together. ∞

MATERIALS:

Book Part	Construction Material	# to Cut	Cutting size
Front and back covers	Medium weight board	2	2-1/4" x 10"
Coverings	Decorative paper	2	3-1/2" x 11"
Pages	Heavy cover weight paper	1	9-3/4" x 12"
Page inserts	Parchment paper	5	1-1/2" x 9-1/4"
Binding cord	Thin gold cord	1	18"

Additional material: Black glass bead

CHAPTER 6

PAPERBACK JOURNALS

Journals are very useful books, and these projects prove they can be beautiful as well. Use them to keep records (such as travel expenses) or to record your experiences or innermost thoughts by keeping diaries. Several types are given here to make your own special journals.

These are called paperback journals because there are no heavy cover boards used in these books.

CORRUGATED CARDBOARD JOURNALS

These simple paperback journals are the easiest and least expensive journals to produce. You will be able to create many different styles and sizes with this method. The fine, colored corrugated card in sheets is the best choice for the covers. When the journal is finished, the ribs of the corrugated card should run vertically. I like to use soft, handmade papers for the pages such as Lokta from Nepal or a natural text weight paper from Japan such as Kasuiri or Kozoshi. Flyleaves should be cut from a natural paper that is a slightly heavier weight than the paper used for the pages. Use a natural binding cord such as twisted hemp cord or raffia to bind your book together. Finish off your journal with a charm to accent the front cover.

MATERIALS:

Finished size: 5-1/2" x 8"

Book Part	Construction Material	# to Cut	Cutting size
Front & back covers and spine	Corrugated card	1	8" x 11"
Endpapers	Decorative paper	1	7-3/4" x 10-3/4"
Flyleaves	Natural Japanese paper	2	5-1/8" x 7-3/4"
Pages	Natural Japanese paper	30	5-1/8" x 7-3/4"
Binding cord	Raffia	1	36"

Binding guide: 1" x 8"; 7 holes, 1" apart

HERE'S HOW:

The cover material does not need to be covered with decorative paper, simply cut the corrugated card stock to size and assemble as follows.

1. Glue the end paper to the inside of the corrugated card piece, leaving a 1/4" border of card showing all around the end paper. Be careful as you rub-down the paper or you will flatten the ribbing on the corrugated card.
2. Knock-down the pages and place inside the cover. Align the stack of papers to the right hand side of the cover, square over the end paper piece.
3. Fold over the front of the cover and clamp to hold the book together. With the binding guide, mark the holes for binding with pencil.
4. With an awl, make the holes for the binding. Since the holes need to be small, the awl should be all that is needed to make holes, rather than using a hole punch. Push hard to make a clean hole through to the back, then turn the journal over and enlarge the holes by piercing them through from the back.
5. With a large tapestry needle threaded with the binding cord, bind the journal together using the binding technique of your choice.

VARIATIONS

Save all your paper scraps when making these journals so you can create a variety of sizes and shapes. Small pocket note books or long books to hold lists can all be useful. You can vary the look of the journal by folding over the front cover only halfway to create a different style of writing pad. Look for the wavy style of corrugated card in art and rubber stamp stores for a special look. ∞

BINDING GUIDE - ACTUAL SIZE

CORRUGATED CARDBOARD JOURNALS

Shown here are more corrugated cardboard journals. If you can't find colored corrugated material, the cardboard can be easily painted with acrylic paints. Use gloss acrylic paints or spray with a glossy finish after paint has dried to give more protection to the paint. A simple embellishment on the front is all that is needed to make these books very special.

FABRIC TRAVEL JOURNAL

Pictured on page 82

This journal, covered entirely with a printed cotton fabric, has a closed spine with a protective flap to create a distinct book design. The covers, hinges, and flaps are covered at the same time, producing the spine and cover all in one piece. A thin matboard is used for the cover boards, hinges, and flap, making it a flexible, thin paperback-like cover. Solid colored cotton fabric is fused to the inside for the endpapers and a lightweight 20 lb. bond paper is used for the pages. Eyelets reinforce the holes and black leather lacing is used for the binding. The journal also includes a built-in ribbon book mark with a pocket watch charm on the end. This journal is a little more challenging than the other projects, but the finished appearance is well worth the effort.

Finished size: 5-3/4" x 9"

MATERIALS:

Book Part	Construction Material	# to Cut	Cutting size
Front cover	Medium weight board	1	5-3/4" x 7-1/2"
Back cover	Medium weight board	1	5-3/4" x 8-1/2"
Hinges A and B	Medium weight board	2	1" x 5-3/4"
Hinges C and D	Medium weight board	2	5/16" x 5-3/4"
Flap	Medium weight board	1	5-3/4" x 2"
Covering (back cover)	Printed cotton fabric with fusible adhesive	1	8" x 15"
Covering (front cover)	Printed cotton fabric with fusible adhesive	1	8" x 10-1/2"
Endpaper (back cover)	Cotton fabric with fusible adhesive	1	11" x 5-1/2"
Endpaper (front cover)	Cotton fabric with fusible adhesive	1	8-1/4" x 5-1/2"
Pages	20 lb. bond paper	100	8-1/2" x 5-1/2"
Binding cord	Leather lacing	3	8"
Flap closure	Leather lacing	1	10"
Bookmark	Black grosgrain ribbon	1	10"

Binding guide: 1" x 5-3/4"; 3 holes, 2" apart

HERE'S HOW:

1. With a pencil lightly label (on the fronts of the pieces) all the cover, hinges, and flap matboard pieces.
2. Trim the ends of the flap board piece and the back cover endpaper piece as shown in Fig. 1.
3. Spray the backs of all the covers, hinges, and flap board pieces with spray adhesive. This will prevent the pieces from shifting while fusing to the covers.
4. Lay the back covering piece on the ironing board with the fusible adhesive side up. Following Fig. 2, lay out the hinges, cover, and flap board pieces, sticky side down.
5. Fuse the fabric sides to the backside of the board pieces. Turn the entire piece over and fuse the fabric to the pieces.
6. Repeat with the front cover, following Fig. 3 for placement of the cover and hinge.

continued on next page

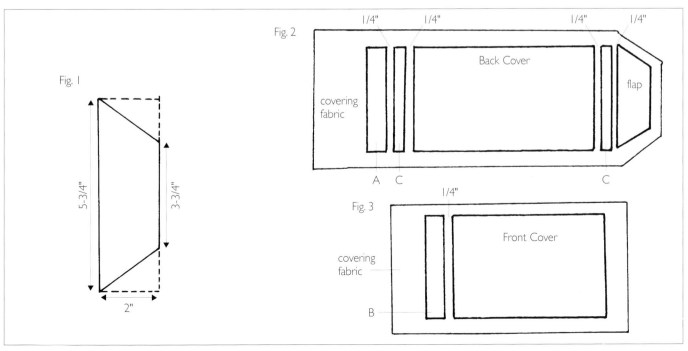

Fig. 1

Fig. 2

Fig. 3

Fabric Travel Journal (cont.)

7. Fuse the end paper fabric pieces to the inside of the front and back covers.

8. Following Fig. 4 and using the eyelet hole tool, make the holes in the covers as indicated. Affix eyelets on all the holes.

9. Make the holes in the pages using the binding guide for placement.

10. Knock-down the pages and place them in the back cover, aligning the page holes with the holes in the back cover. Bring the back cover end hinge over and align the holes to the front cover holes. Clamp to hold. The flap holes should line up with the holes in the front cover for the leather lacing closure piece.

11. Use the three pieces of leather lacing and thread through the binding holes. Double knot to hold.

12. Thread the 10" piece of leather lacing through the two holes on the front cover and through the flap to close the book.

13. Glue the grosgrain ribbon bookmark to the inside of the back cover for the bookmark. ∞

BINDING GUIDE -
ACTUAL SIZE

Fig. 4

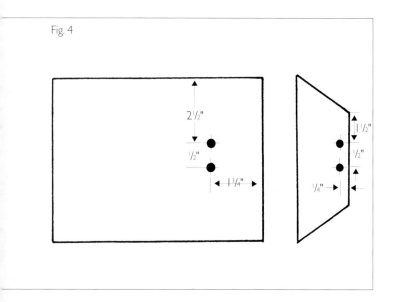

FABRIC-COVERED DIARY

This is a fabric covered journal constructed with one cover piece that wraps around the pages and forms its own spine. The cover is made from fabric covered pastel paper for a flexible, paperback book. The end paper is solid colored fabric, and the decorative pieces at the fore edge are cut from the same material.

Finished size: 5" x 8-1/2"

MATERIALS:

Book Part	Construction Material	# to Cut	Cutting size
Front & back covers and spine	Fabric laminated with pastel paper	1	5-3/4" x 18"
Endpapers	Fabric with fusible adhesive	1	4-1/2" x 16-3/4"
Decorative end pieces	Fabric with fusible adhesive	2	1-1/2" x 5-3/4"
Flyleaves	Natural handmade paper	2	4-1/2" x 8"
Pages	Ivory 20 lb. bond	80-100	4-1/2" x 8"
Binding cord	Leather lacing	1	20"
Book closure	Leather lacing	1	10"

Binding guide: 1" x 4-3/4"; 4 holes, 1" apart

HERE'S HOW:

1. Mark, score, and fold over a 1/2" hem around the entire cover piece. Trim the corners and glue the hem down. Your cover will now measure 4-3/4" x 17".
2. Mark and score the inside of your cover as indicated in Fig.1.
3. Fuse the decorative ends onto the short edges of the cover. Let 1/2" show on the outside of the cover, fold in the edges,

then fold and fuse the other half over to the back.

4. Fuse the endpaper material to the inside of the cover.

5. Make the holes for the binding cord using the binding guide and the hole making tool that comes with the eyelets. Also make a hole at the ends of the cover in the middle of the decorative strip. Reinforce all the holes on the cover with eyelets.

6. Make the holes in the pages. Knock-down the pages and place in the cover.

7. Bind the book with the binding cord. Thread the 10" piece of cord through the holes at the fore edge to close the book. ∾

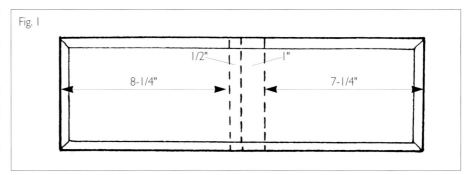

Fig. I

8-1/4"   1/2"   1"   7-1/4"

BINDING GUIDE - ACTUAL SIZE

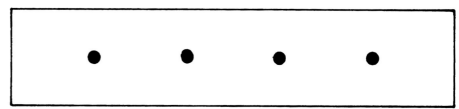

CHAPTER 7

WOOD COVERED BOOKS

The ancient Greeks kept written records on wax covered wooden tablets that were hinged together with leather. This early wood covered book was called a codex and was the earliest form of what we now call a book. Wood makes an effective cover for the pages of a book. It is easy to construct, strong, and makes an excellent surface for many types of decoration. One of the wooden book designs presented here is made from a purchased album cover and the other has been crafted from thin sheets of plywood.

CABIN JOURNAL

This is created using a purchased wooden album. This wooden journal in which to record your vacation highlights for years to come has a rustic style that's perfect for a mountain cabin or ski lodge.

MATERIALS:

6" x 9" wooden album cover (comes complete with brass hinges and expandable posts for adding extra pages).
Paper for inside pages, natural, handmade paper with a rustic look, cut to 5-3/4" x 8-1/2" (cut the pages to fit the album you have purchased).

HERE'S HOW:

1. I prefer to decorate the cover before assembling the journal. Stain the covers (both front and back, inside and out) with an oak colored stain.
2. When dry, sand with a fine grade sandpaper for a smooth surface and to bring out the wood grain.
3. Stamp with an oak leaf stamp and thermal emboss with gold powder.
4. Stamp "Cabin Days" with a rubber stamp and thermal emboss with black powder.
5. Acorn charms and antiqued oak leaf charms are glued onto the cover for accents.
6. Punch the holes in the pages to line up with the drilled holes in the cover. Align the paper at the left side, flush with the edge of the book. You will have a 1/4" margin at fore edge. Center the paper top to bottom so you have a 1/4" margin at both top and bottom.
7. Put the journal together with the provided hardware. ∞

WEDDING PHOTO ALBUM

This elegant album will protect your treasured wedding photographs for generations. The carved wooden ornaments are glued on, and the surface is painted and antiqued for an exquisite treasure.

Finished size: 8-3/4" x 11-1/4"

MATERIALS:

Book Part	Construction Material	# to Cut	Cutting size
Front and back covers	1/4" thick plywood	2	11-1/4" x 8-3/4"
Hinge hardware	Brass hinges and screws	2	3/4" size
Endpapers	Gold filigree printed paper	2	8-1/2" x 9-1/2"
Pages	Cream pastel paper	15	11-3/4" x 8-1/4"
Front cover accents	Wooden molding pieces		
Binding cord	Cream satin cord	1	16"

Binding guide: 1-1/2" x 8-3/4"; 2 holes, 4-1/2" apart

Binding Guide Diagram

1-1/2"   4-1/2"   2-1/8"

8-3/4"

HERE'S HOW:

1. With the piece of plywood that will be the front cover, cut the board 1-1/2" from the spine edge to create the hinge piece.
2. Glue the wooden molding pieces to the front cover and let dry.
3. Basecoat and stencil the front cover. I antiqued the covers and hinge piece by first basecoating, inside and out, with a metallic gold acrylic paint. When dry, rub with a piece of paraffin wax. Wax where the piece would normally get wear over the years—at the edges and the surface of the decorative molding pieces. Paint the covers with cream acrylic paint, leaving the insides of the covers and edges gold. When dry, sand the covers with fine sandpaper. Where you waxed, the gold paint will show through giving the piece an antique look. If you wish, add a little stenciling with gold acrylic paint for added accent.

4. Construct the front cover by adding on the hinge hardware and connecting the hinge to the front cover.
5. Mark, score, and fold 1" over at the spine edge of each page piece. Your pages are now 10- 3/4" x 8-1/4". This will hold the bulk of the photographs without effecting the overall appearance of the album.
6. Glue the endpapers into the inside of the covers, aligning with the fore edge.

7. To prevent the book from splaying, glue the covers and each page together with a small amount of glue at the spine edge. Clamp to hold while drying.
8. Drill the binding holes into the covers and pages using the binding guide. Glue a gold eyelet into each binding hole.
9. Using the binding cord, bind the cover and pages together. A decorative gold bow is glued to the hinge for an elegant touch. ∞

Chapter 8

CLOSED SPINE BOOKS

The closed spine style book is based on a simple slab style of binding which is Japanese in origin. I refer to these books as "closed spine books" because the spine material is cut in one piece and is wrapped around the spine edge of both covers, enclosing the pages. The covers are hinged to allow easy opening of the journal and the pages are laced inside with a binding cord. Various designs are offered here with a few sizes from which to choose.

BASIC CLOSED SPINE BOOK

The dimensions for this basic design are good for journals and small photo albums. You can create guest books, recipe books, or books to use for a collection of poems.

Finished size: 6" x 9-1/4"

MATERIALS:

BINDING GUIDE - ACTUAL SIZE

Book Part	Construction Material	# to Cut	Cutting size
Front and back covers	Medium weight board	2	6" x 7-1/2"
Hinges	Medium weight board	2	1-1/4" x 6"
Coverings for covers	Decorative paper	2	9-1/2" x 8"
Spine cover	Fabric or paper ribbon with fusible webbing	1	5" x 14"
Endpapers	Decorative paper	2	7-1/4" x 5-3/4"
Flyleaves	Decorative paper	2	8-3/4" x 5-3/4"
Pages	20 lb. bond	40	8-3/4" x 5-3/4"
Binding cord	1/8" satin ribbon	1	30"

Binding guide: 1-1/2" x 6"; 5 holes, 1" apart

HERE'S HOW:

1. Glue the decorative paper of your choice to the front and back cover boards.
2. Assemble the spine and fuse the covers and hinges into the spine, following the general directions for a closed spine in the "Bookbinding Techniques" section.
3. Glue the endpapers to the inside of the front and back covers.
4. Knock-down the pages and flyleaves and place into the cover and spine. Clamp down to hold.
5. Using the binding guide, mark the binding holes with an awl. Drill through the spine and pages. Without removing the clamps, sew the binding cord through the drilled holes to hold your book together.
6. Remove clamps and add any additional surface decorations. ∾

Guest Book (Shown in the Photo)

This book is covered with a Victorian style wrapping paper. The spine is constructed from antiqued burgundy paper ribbon. The pages are ivory 20 lb. bond paper and the fly leaves and endpapers are cut from a piece of antiqued paper. The cover is decoupaged with antiqued labels and a cherub motif. The binding cord is a thin gold and burgundy grosgrain ribbon.

Metallic Silver Book

This is a striking design using silver leaf to gild the covers and metallic silver paper with a sticky backing to form the spine and decorative edges. Silver and gold metallic paper with an adhesive backing are available in craft shops and fine art stores. The endpapers are cut from hand marbled papers in a soft gray color on white paper for a smoky effect. The pages are cut from gray marbled 20 lb. bond paper. The binding cord is thin silver cord. The front dimensional design is drawn with a glue gun then gilded with the silver leaf for an amazing melted metal effect. ∾

LARGE SCRAPBOOK

This large version of the Closed Spine Book is perfect for a memory scrapbook. The cover boards are covered with a handmade cover weight rag and rice paper. The spine is a printed cotton with fusible adhesive, and the decorative corners are cut from the same fused fabric. The endpapers are cut from a beautiful gold filigree paper from India. The pages are cut from a Lokta and corn silk paper from Nepal. Strips of thicker pastel paper are cut and placed between each page so you can glue in your memory items without the book becoming distorted from the extra bulk. The book is bound with a 1-1/2" width gold ribbon, and the front cover is adorned with a large gold rose charm.

Finished size: 8" x 12-1/4"

MATERIALS:

Book Part	Construction Material	# to Cut	Cutting size
Front and back covers	Medium weight board	2	8" x 10"
Hinges	Medium weight board	2	2" x 8"
Coverings for covers	Decorative paper	2	10" x 12"
Spine cover	Fabric with fusible webbing	1	7" x 22"
Decorative corners	Fabric with fusible webbing	4	3" x 3"
Endpapers	Decorative paper	2	7-3/4" x 9-3/4"
Flyleaves	Decorative paper	2	8-3/4" x 5-3/4"
Pages	Lightweight handmade paper	30	7-3/4" x 11-3/4"
Page inserts	Pastel paper	28	7-3/4" x 1-1/2"
Binding cord	Wide metallic ribbon	1	36"

Binding guide: 2" x 8"; 2 holes, 3" apart

HERE'S HOW:

Follow the general directions for the Basic Closed Spine Book with the following additional steps:

1. Remember to place the decorative corners onto the covers before the endpapers are glued in.
2. Knock-down the pages, clamp at the fore edge, then slip in a page insert strip between each sheet at the spine edge. Carefully place between the covers and clamp to hold while drilling holes and binding with the binding cord.

BINDING GUIDE - ACTUAL SIZE

GARDEN NOTES

The small size of this journal works well for books that can be slipped into a pocket or purse for quick access in jotting down notes. The cover boards are covered with a handmade paper infused with grass clippings, and the spine material is paper ribbon with fusible adhesive. The endpapers are cut from handmade spattered paper. The flyleaves are the same paper used to cover the book. The pages are cut from green pastel paper. The binding cord is garden twine with a twig woven in for decoration. The front cover is embellished with copper colored charms, pressed flowers, and scraps of handmade papers. A simple book mark can be made from a copper plant tag with a copper charm.

Finished size: 5-1/4" x 5"

MATERIALS:

Book Part	Construction Material	# to Cut	Cutting size
Front and back covers	Medium weight board	2	4" x 5"
Hinges	Medium weight board	2	1" x 5"
Coverings for covers	Decorative paper	2	6" x 7"
Spine cover	Paper ribbon with fusible adhesive	1	4-1/2" x 11"
Endpapers	Decorative paper	2	3-3/4" x 4-3/4"
Flyleaves	Decorative paper	2	4-3/4" x 5"
Pages	Lightweight handmade paper	30	4-3/4" x 5"
Binding cord	Garden twine	1	26"

Binding guide: 1" x 5"; 5 holes, 3/4" apart

HERE'S HOW:

Follow the general directions for the Basic Closed Spine Book.

BINDING GUIDE - ACTUAL SIZE

CHAPTER 9

OPEN SPINE BOOKS

The Open Spine Book is very similar to the Closed Spine Book except the spine is formed in two parts; the spine edge is open and the pages can be seen. This technique is a little easier than the Closed Spine Book and looks very similar when finished. Various sizes and designs are offered here.

BASIC OPEN SPINE BOOK

Finished size: 6" x 8-3/4"

MATERIALS:

Book Part	Construction Material	# to Cut	Cutting size
Front and back covers	Medium weight board	2	6" x 7-1/2"
Hinges	Medium weight board	2	1" x 6"
Coverings for covers	Decorative paper	2	8" x 9-1/2"
Spine cover	Fabric or paper ribbon with fusible adhesive	2	4-1/2" x 8"
Endpapers	Decorative paper	2	7-1/4" x 5-3/4"
Flyleaves	Decorative paper	2	8-1/2" x 5-3/4"
Pages	20 lb. bond	40	8-1/2" x 5-3/4"
Binding cord	1/8" ribbon or thin cord	1	30"

Binding guide: 1" x 6"; 4 holes, 1-1/2" apart

HERE'S HOW:

1. Glue the decorative paper of your choice to the front and back cover boards.
2. Assemble the spine pieces and fuse to the covers and hinges, following general directions for constructing an Open Spine Book in the "Bookbinding Techniques" section.
3. Glue the endpapers to the inside of the front and back covers.
4. Knock-down the pages and flyleaves and place into the cover and spine. Clamp down to hold.
5. Using the binding guide, mark the binding holes with an awl. Drill through the spine and pages. Without removing the clamps, sew the binding cord through the drilled holes to hold your book together.
6. Remove clamps and add any additional surface decorations. ∽

BOOKS SHOWN IN THE PHOTO

Marbled Paper Journal

This journal is covered with a beautiful piece of hand marbled paper in tones of white, gray, and blue. The spine material is gray book-linen cloth, and the pages are cut from gray marbled 20 lb. bond. The flyleaves and endpapers are cut from a midnight blue Chautara Lokta paper from Nepal. The binding cord is thin white satin ribbon with beads at the end to embellish.

Natural Leaf Journal

This journal is covered with a cover weight natural paper with straw and long plant fibers. The spines are made by gluing on pieces of tan ultra suede. The pages are cut from a 20 lb. bond paper with a ivory parchment finish. The flyleaves are a handmade paper with straw fibers in a text weight to match the cover. Endpapers are a hand decorated piece of paper with a leaf motif. The binding cord is natural raffia that has been stained a dark brown.

BINDING GUIDE - ACTUAL SIZE

BABY BRAG BOOK

This fabric covered photo album is the perfect size to hold photographs of your beloved little baby. The cover board is padded with a polyester batting and the cover and spine are constructed with a single piece of fused fabric. I designed the brag book for a little girl, but you can easily adorn the front with blue buttons and ribbons for a little boy. The front cover is embellished with ribbons and lace corners (placed on before gluing in the endpapers to hide the ends), small crocheted medallions, buttons, pearls, and antiqued charms. The pages are folded over 1" at the spine edge to accommodate the bulk of the photographs.

Finished size: 8-1/2" x 5"

MATERIALS:

Book Part	Construction Material	# to Cut	Cutting size
Front and back covers	Heavy weight board	2	5" x 7"
Hinges	Heavy weight board	2	1-1/4" x 5"
Covering and spine	White fabric with fusible adhesive	2	7" x 13"
Cover padding	Thin polyester batting	2	5" x 7"
Hinge padding	Thin polyester batting	2	1-1/4" x 5"
Endpapers	White pastel paper	2	6-3/4" x 4-3/4"
Flyleaves	White pastel paper	2	8" x 4-3/4"
Pages	Pink pastel paper	40	9" x 4-3/4"
Binding cord	Thin white satin ribbon	1	26"
Corner accents	3" wide lace ribbon	4	3" x 3"
Ribbon accents	Variety of thin ribbons and lace edging	3	7"

Binding guide: 5" x 1"; 4 holes, 1" apart

HERE'S HOW:

1. After the pages have been cut, mark, score, and fold over each piece 1" at the spine edge. Your pages will now be 8" x 4-3/4".
2. With white glue, tack the polyester batting to the front of the cover boards and the hinges. Place the padded covers and hinges, padded side down, onto the prepared fabric and fuse to create the covers.
3. Glue on the lace corner accents. Glue the decorative ribbons on the cover, bringing the extra lengths to the inside of the front cover.
4. Glue the endpapers onto the inside of the covers.
5. Knock-down the pages and place on the back cover with the folded edge at the spine edge. Place the front cover on top and clamp into place.
6. Punch the binding holes and bind your book together with the white satin ribbon. Finish embellishing your photo album by gluing on the buttons, bows, medallions, pearls, and charms with white craft glue.

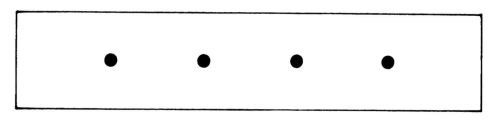

BOTANICAL JOURNAL

The Botanical Journal is designed to hold loose sheets of pressed flowers and has no side binding. The covers and pages are held together with straps made from black grosgrain ribbon and plastic fasteners. Or, you can use wide elastic ribbon to hold your book together. The design also works well for holding a collection of 5" x 7" photographs on black pastel paper. The 5-3/4" x 8-1/2" cover boards are cut from a heavy weight board and covered with wrapping paper with natural motifs. The pages are handmade Lokta paper from Nepal. The natural paper gives a marvelous mounting surface for the pressed flower collections. Endpapers are natural kraft paper and the journal is labeled with a piece of torn paper and a fern charm.

FAUX LEATHER PHOTO ALBUM

Pictured on pages 104-105

This old fashion style photo album uses the faux leather technique to give it a refined appearance. The faux leather is painted with black acrylic paint which helps to give it strength. The front cover has a panel covered with a faux embossed leather paper and a window is cut out for the album title. The pages are folded at the spine edge to accommodate the bulk of the photographs. A printed paper from Italy is used for endpapers. Black velvet ribbon is used for the binding cord.

Finished size: 11-3/4" x 7-1/4"

MATERIALS:

Book Part	Construction Material	# to Cut	Cutting size
Front and back covers	Heavy weight board	2	10-3/4" x 7-1/4"
Hinges	Heavy weight board	2	3/4" x 7-1/4"
Covering and spine	Faux leather paper	2	15-1/2" x 9-1/4"
Cover panel	Medium weight board	1	5" x 9"
Covering for cover panel	Faux embossed leather paper	1	7" x 11"
Endpapers	Decorative paper	2	10-1/2" x 7"
Pages	Black pastel paper	10	12" x 7"
Binding cord	Thin velvet ribbon	1	20"

Binding guide: 7-1/4" x 3/4"; 2 holes, 4-1/2" apart

HERE'S HOW:

1. Cover the front and back covers and hinge pieces, following the directions in the Basic Open Spine Book.
2. Cut a 4" x 1" window out of the center of the cover panel piece.
3. Cover the panel piece with the faux embossed leather. On a scrap piece of black pastel paper, write the title of the album with a gold paint pen. Glue to the back of the panel piece, centering the lettering in the cutout window.
4. Glue the panel piece to the front cover.
5. Prepare the pages by marking, scoring, and folding the spine edges of the pages 1/2" over. The pages will now be 11-1/2" x 7".
6. To prevent the book from splaying glue the covers and each page together with a small amount of glue at the spine edge. Clamp to hold while drying.
7. Drill the holes into the covers and pages and bind together with the velvet ribbon. ∞

BINDING GUIDE - ACTUAL SIZE

CHAPTER 10

ENVELOPE BOOKS

These books use envelopes for the pages and are constructed with an expandable folded spine so you can fill the "pages" with small treasures for a unique gift-filled booklet. A few of the possible gifts to put in the envelope pages include: scented bath salts, flavored teas, recipes, stickers, stamps, handmade gift tags and labels, seeds, small ornaments, candy, theater passes, or spice and herb blends. You can also use the envelope book design to create a handy book to place receipts for expenses while traveling. All the envelope book projects have 1/2" pleats for the accordion-folded spine.

BASIC ENVELOPE BOOK

Finished Size: 5" x 7"

MATERIALS:

Book Part	Construction Material	# to Cut	Cutting size
Front and back covers	Medium weight board	2	5" x 7"
Covering papers	Decorative paper	2	7" x 9"
Paper spine	Pastel paper	1	5" x 8"
Endpapers	Pastel paper to match spine	2	4-3/4" x 6-3/4"
Pages	Envelopes	6	6-1/2" x 4-1/2"
Flyleaf	20 lb. bond paper	1	6-1/2" x 4-1/2"
Closure ties	Ribbon	2	12"

HERE'S HOW:

1. Cover the cover boards with the decorative paper.
2. Construct the spine by marking, scoring, and folding 1/2" accordion pleats with the bone folder.
3. Label, decorate, or cut the envelope pages if called for in the individual project instructions.
4. Flatten out the spine and, using a glue stick, glue the edge of the envelope into each pleat. If adding a flyleaf, glue it in with the first envelope page. Clamp to hold while drying with a large bull clip.
5. Glue the end pleats onto the covers at the spine edge. Use a strong craft glue for this task, and use the bull clip to clamp while drying.
6. Glue in closure ties at the fore edge.
7. Glue in the endpapers. You are now ready to decorate your cover to finish your gift book.

Instructions for books shown—
Tea Collection Book, Business Travel Book,
and Seed Saver File are on the following
pages. Seed Saver File instructions are on
page 110

TEA COLLECTION BOOK

The Tea Collection envelope book is covered with a natural handmade paper with straw fibers, and the spine and endpapers are cut from mocha brown colored pastel paper. I used translucent parchment paper envelopes, but ordinary white or kraft envelopes would work equally as well. Decorative labels are placed on the front of each envelope. The front cover is decorated with a label made from the pastel paper and a skeleton leaf. The closure ties are two-tone gold and brown satin ribbon. Each envelope contains enough flavored tea to make a pot full. Write the directions for making the perfect pot of tea on the flyleaf.

BUSINESS TRAVEL BOOK

This is a handy envelope book to carry receipts for your expenses on a business trip. Label the kraft paper envelopes with headings such as "meals," "local transport," "entertainment," "lodging," and "misc. expenses." The envelopes are 5-1/2" x 8-1/2" cut down to size, and the openings are at the fore edge of the book for easy access. The cover boards are covered with an olive colored Jerusalem Java paper and the spine is cut from card weight white paper. The closure ties are a sheer olive colored ribbon. Endpapers are cut from wrapping paper, and the cover is decorated with scraps of handmade paper and a key.

MATERIALS:

Book Part	Construction Material	# to Cut	Cutting size
Front and back covers	Medium weight board	2	4-1/2" x 5-1/2"
Covering for covers	Handmade paper	2	6-1/2" x 7-1/2"
Paper spine	White card	1	5-1/2" x 8"
Endpapers	Decorative paper	2	4-1/4" x 5-1/4"
Pages	Kraft envelopes	6	4-1/2" x 5-1/2"
Closure ties	Olive green sheer ribbon	2	12"

Finished Size: 4-1/2" x 5-1/2"

HERE'S HOW:

Follow the instructions for the Basic Envelope Book

SEED SAVER FILE

The Seed Saver File uses all the same skills and techniques as the envelope book but has two spines on each side to create a handy little file. It was designed to hold small packages of seeds but could also hold recipe cards, cards with addresses and phone numbers, or business cards. The file is lined with fabric for durability, and the envelope compartments automatically open up when the file is opened. Accent the front with a charm to finish.

Finished size: 4-1/2" x 5-1/2"

MATERIALS:

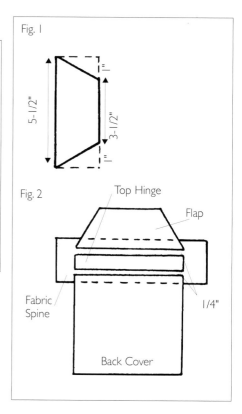

Fig. 1

Fig. 2

Top Hinge

Flap

Fabric Spine

1/4"

Back Cover

Book Part	Construction Material	# to Cut	Cutting size
Front, back covers	Medium weight board	2	4-1/4" x 5-1/2"
Coverings for covers	Decorative wrapping paper	2	6" x 7-1/2"
Covering for flap	Decorative wrapping paper	1	7-1/2" x 5"
Hinge	Medium weight board	1	1/2" x 5-1/2"
Flap	Medium weight board	1	3" x 5-1/2"
Paper spines	Cream colored pastel paper	2	4-1/4" x 10"
Fabric top spine	Cotton fabric with fusible adhesive	1	2-1/2" x 7"
Front endpaper	Cotton fabric with fusible adhesive	1	5-1/4" x 4"
Back endpaper	Cotton fabric with fusible adhesive	1	5-1/4" x 8-1/4"
Pages	5-1/2" x 8-1/2" kraft envelopes, cut down into pockets	8	3-3/4" x 5-1/2"
Closure ties	Thin green satin ribbon	2	12"

HERE'S HOW:

1. Trim the flap piece and the back endpaper piece as shown in Fig. 1.
2. Cover the cover boards and the flap piece with the decorative paper.
3. Construct the back cover by centering the hinge piece, back cover, and flap piece on the fabric top spine as shown in Fig.2. Fold over the fabric on the sides and fuse the boards to the top spine.
4. Glue the closure ties to the top and the bottom of the back cover piece. Fuse the endpapers onto the back and front covers.
5. Construct the paper spines with 1/2" accordion pleats.
6. Glue the envelope pockets into the pleats. Do one side, clamp, and let the glue dry. Then glue into the second pleated side.
7. To finish, glue the end pleats to the front and back covers and clamp to hold while drying.

FRAGRANT BATH CRYSTALS BOOK

The Fragrant Spring Bath Crystal Envelope Giftbook is a beautiful and fragrant gift that would look exquisite on a shelf or counter in the bathroom. The covering paper is cut from a sheet of printed paper from Italy. The spine and endpapers are cut from a deep teal pastel paper. The envelope pages are glassine paper envelopes, but you can substitute with ordinary envelopes. The parchment paper flyleaf holds the directions on how to enjoy the bath crystals. A 2-1/4" wide sheer ribbon with a gold edge is used as the closure tie, and the front cover is decorated with a gold edged label and a rose charm.

Spring Bath Crystals Recipe

1 cup Epsom salts
1 cup large coarse salt
10 to 20 drops rain fragrance oil
10 drops food coloring

Place the salts in a large bowl and mix well. Take out about 1/2 cup in a small bowl. Add the drops of fragrance and color to this smaller amount and mix well. Add the blended mixture to the large bowl, a little at a time, until you are pleased with the color strength. Pour your salts in a glass jar with a tight fitting lid. Store and shake everyday for one week before packaging. Place 1/4 cup of the bath crystals into each envelope page.

Directions for use:
Draw a warm bath and add 1/4 cup of the fragrant salts to the running water. Hop in and relax, inhaling deeply to experience the soothing qualities of aromatherapy.

CHAPTER 11

STICKY PAD NOTEBOOKS

These simple little note pads are perfect for office gifts or stocking stuffers during the holiday season. They use the little sticky note pads available in office supple stores in a variety of sizes and colors.

SQUARE NOTE PADS

This design uses the 3" square note pad size and I like the new safari color packages for their soft, subtle designer colors.

Finished size: 3-1/8" x 3-1/8"

MATERIALS:

Book Part	Construction Material	# to Cut	Cutting size
Front and back covers	Medium weight board	2	3-1/8" x 3-1/8"
Covering for covers	Hand decorated paper	2	4-1/2" x 4-1/2"
Spine	Ultra suede	1	1-3/4" x 3-1/2"
Pages	Sticky note pad	1	3" x 3"
Endpapers	Pages from the sticky note pad	2	3" x 3"

HERE'S HOW:

1. Cover the cover boards with the decorative paper. Glue the end papers into the inside of the covers.
2. Lay the ultra suede hinge on right side down on your work surface. Place the glue along the long sides. Place the covered boards right side down on the glued edge with a 1/2" overlap (Fig.1). Trim the excess ultra suede so the spine is flush with the boards.
3. Let dry before taking off the backing sheet from the sticky pad and placing on the back cover board, aligning with the endpaper piece.
4. Finish by decorating the front with a small charm. ∽

VARIATION

Instead of covering the matboard pieces with decorative paper, use the layered embossed method to give an interesting finish to your little note books.

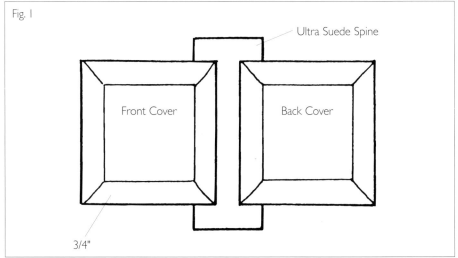

Fig. I

Ultra Suede Spine

Front Cover

Back Cover

3/4"

Corrugated Spine Books

This is a very quick and easy notebook that can fit in small places like pockets, briefcases, and school bags.

Finished size: 3-1/4" x 5-1/4"

Materials:

Book Part	Construction Material	# to Cut	Cutting size
Front and back covers	Medium weight board	2	3-1/8" x 5-1/4"
Coverings for covers	Decorative paper	2	5" x 7"
Spine	Corrugated card	1	2-3/4" x 5-1/4"
Endpapers	Decorative paper	2	3" x 5"
Pages	Pad of 3" x 5" sticky notes	1 pad	3" x 5"
Closure cord	Raffia	2	10"

Here's How:

1. Cover the cover boards with the decorative paper.
2. Lay the corrugated card spine on your work surface, right side down. With the bone folder, mark and score two folds as indicated in Fig.1. Apply glue on each side of the folds and adhere covers in place.
3. Glue the closure cords in the middle of the inside of the covers. Glue in the endpapers, the long edge right up against the spine edge of the cover.
4. Remove the backing paper from the sticky note pad and place the pad alongside the spine edge of the back cover, on top of the endpaper.

Projects Pictured

Natural Paper Example: It is covered with hazelnut colored Jerusalem Java handmade paper, the spine is cut from corrugated card. The pages are a purchased pad of 3" x 5" sticky notes that can be replaced when finished. The raffia to close the notebook is glued on the front and back covers before the green bond paper endpapers are glued in. A simple seal decorates the front cover.

Metallic Examples: These funky little note pads have covers decorated with gold, silver, and copper gilded surfaces with dimensional gilded motifs. The books are then antiqued with acrylic paint. The back covers and edges are painted with matching acrylic paint to finish off the books.

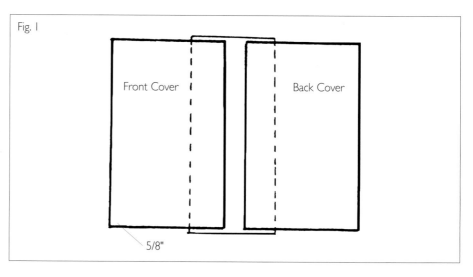

Fig. 1

Front Cover   Back Cover

5/8"

Message Pad

This project uses bookbinding skills and techniques, and the pad is a large sticky note pad. The ultra suede piece is a holder for a matching pen. Charm corners and wooden knobs help to make this message pad a very sophisticated gift item.

Finished size: 6" x 6-1/2" x 1"

Materials:

Book Part	Construction Material	# to Cut	Cutting size
Base	Heavy weight board	1	6" x 6-1/2"
Covering for base	Decorative paper	1	8" x 8-1/2"
Covering for bottom of base	Handmade paper	1	5-1/2" x 6-1/4"
Covering for pen	Decorative paper to match base	1	4-1/2" x 1-1/2"
Message pad	Sticky note pad	1	3" x 5"
Message pad decorative base	Handmade paper	1	3" x 5"
Pen holder	Ultra suede	1	3" x 1-3/4"
Feet	Wooden knobs	4	3/4"
Decorative corners	Metallic corner charms	4	3/4"

Here's How:

1. Cut a small window into the base piece following the placement in Fig.1.
2. Cover the base with the decorative paper, cutting out the window. Glue the ultra suede piece into the window with 1/2" piece on each side glued down to the back. The resulting loop should be large enough to hold the pen.
3. Glue the covering for the back of the base in place. Glue the decorative message pad base to the top, using the placement directions in Fig.1.
4. Paint the wooden knobs to match your chosen decorative paper and glue to the bottom of the base at the four corners. Glue the decorative corner charms in place.
5. For added decoration, stamp and emboss the word "messages" below the message pad.
6. Remove the backing paper from the sticky note pad and place on the decorative pad base. Cover the pen with the decorative paper, and wrap some natural cord around the end for an added decorative touch. ∽

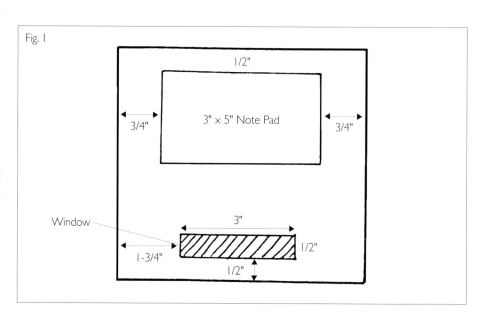

Fig. I

CHAPTER 12

NOVELTY BOOKS

In this chapter you will find some very intriguing little books that are great fun to make and use. When you get to the end of this chapter, I hope you have gained enough skill and inspiration so that your mind is busy thinking about ideas for your own unique style of books. There are so many possibilities.

SEED BOOK

This pretty little book is designed to place in the garden and bloom into a carpet of fragrant wildflowers. The instructions on the inside of the front cover outlines how to cut the binding cord, trim the pages which have been infused with hundreds of wildflower seeds, and fit into plant pots or cut into strips for a floral border in the garden. I used home-made paper with feathery deckle edges for this project but any natural handmade paper can be utilized. It has a simple fold-over design with a sewn spine and is decorated with pressed flowers. It is very important to use a glue that is water soluble to laminate the sheets together. If you use the wrong glue, the seeds will be sealed in and will not germinate. A simple paste of flour and water will work to glue the sheets together.

Finished size: 5" x 6"

MATERIALS:

Book Part	Construction Material	# to Cut	Cutting size
Cover	Cover weight paper laminated with natural petal infused paper	1	9-1/2" x 6"
Pages	Handmade paper with deckle edges	6	6" x 5"
Binding cord	Natural twine	1	18"

Binding guide: 6" x 1/2"; 5 holes, 1" apart

HERE'S HOW:

1. Brush a sheet of the handmade paper with a coat of water soluble glue and sprinkle with a liberal amount of wildflower seeds. Place another sheet on top and laminate the two together. Repeat with the other pages.
2. Score and fold all the pages in half and stack with the spine edges together.
3. Mark the cover 3/8" in from one long edge. This will be the top, bound edge of the book. Score and fold the cover piece at this mark so that you have created a hinge.
4. Place the folded pages into the cover and, using the binding guide, make the holes for the binding cord.
5. Sew the spine up with the binding cord.
6. Glue a label onto the cover and the instructions on the inside front cover. Decorate the cover with a variety of pressed flowers. ∾

Open Book is pictured on page 121

May all your Weeds be WILDFLOWERS

SEED BOOK PATTERNS

Photo copy these onto decorative paper to use in your Seed Book.

May all your Weeds be
WILDFLOWERS

BINDING GUIDE - ACTUAL SIZE

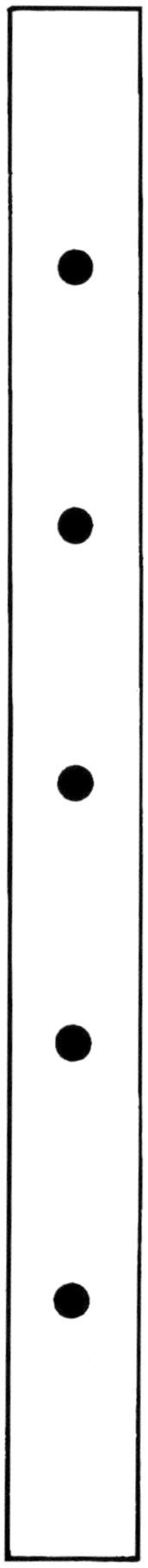

Friends
are the FLOWERS
in the garden of Life

MAKE YOUR BOOK BLOOM!

The pages of your book have been embedded with hundreds of wildflower seeds. Simply cut the binding cord and cut the pages with scissors to fit into clay pots or cut into long strips for the garden. Lay the paper on the top of the soil in a sunny area of your garden and water lightly. Sprinkle on a thin layer of soil. Keep the soil moist and you will be rewarded with a beautiful patch of wildflowers.

The wildflower mixture includes annual chrysanthemum, shasta daisy, scarlet flax, blue flax, primrose, bluebells, black-eyed susan and california poppy.

To: From:

MAKE YOUR BOOK BLOOM!

The pages of your book have been embedded with hundreds of wildflower seeds. Simply cut the binding cord and cut the pages with scissors to fit into clay pots or cut into long strips for the garden. Lay the paper on the top of the soil in a sunny area of your garden and water lightly. Sprinkle on a thin layer of soil. Keep the soil moist and you will be rewarded with a beautiful patch of wildflowers.

The wildflower mixture includes annual chrysanthemum, shasta daisy, scarlet flax, blue flax, primrose, bluebells, black-eyed susan and california poppy.

To: From:

MINIATURE BOOKS

This teeny-tiny book is fully functional and can be used to hold inspirational quotes or very short stories. The book can be worn as a piece of jewelry or it can adorn a key chain. This is a wonderful way to use up little scraps of board and papers that you have saved from other projects.

Finished size: 1-1/2" x 1-3/8"

MATERIALS:

Book Part	Construction Material	# to Cut	Cutting size
Covers	Lightweight board	2	1-1/2" x 1"
Covering for covers	Decorative paper	2	1-3/4" x 2-1/4"
Pages	20 lb. bond paper (the stack should measure 1/4")		1-1/4" x 1-3/8"
Endpapers	Decorative paper	2	1" x 1-1/4"
Spine	Ultra suede	1	1-1/2" x 1-3/8"
Binding cord	Waxed linen thread	1	8"

Binding guide: 1-1/2" x 3/8"; 5 holes, 1/4" apart

HERE'S HOW:

1. Cover the front and back cover boards. Glue in the endpapers to the inside of the covers.
2. Assemble pages and place them between the covers, aligning with the endpapers. About 1/4" of the pages will be sticking out at the spine edge. Clamp the book together with a rubber band to hold in place.
3. Cover the spine with glue and wrap over the exposed pages and the covers. Clamp to hold while drying.
4. When dry, use the binding guide and pierce the holes with an awl. With the binding cord threaded through a needle, sew the spine together.
5. Add a split ring through the top piece of binding cord so you can thread a satin cord for a necklace or a leather cord for a key chain. Adorn your miniature book with a small charm to finish. ◕

BINDING GUIDE - ACTUAL SIZE

Star Ornament Book

This little book with its origami folded pages opens up to make a beautiful star ornament. It can be made with small pieces of leftover decorative papers and is a delightful little gift to bring joy to the recipient. I prefer to use gold and silver metallic self-adhesive paper laminated to a 20 lb. bond. Laminate the two papers together before cutting the required sizes. This makes the ornament very sturdy and gives the inside of the star a good surface on which to write. The book shown includes covers with decorative paper and a gold seal. The cover is decorated with the layered embossed and raised gilded motif techniques.

Finished size: 2" x 2" when the book is closed; 5" x 5" when opened

Materials:

Book Part	Construction Material	# to Cut	Cutting size
Covers	Lightweight board	2	1-7/8" x 1-7/8"
Covering for covers	Decorative paper	2	2-3/4" x 2-3/4"
Pages	20 lb. bond paper laminated to metallic paper	5	3-1/2" x 3-1/2"
Spine and closure tie	Thin 1/8" satin ribbon	1	16"

Here's How:

1. Follow these steps to fold each page: With the metallic side down, fold the page in half (fold A). Unfold and with the metallic side down, fold again in half creating four equal sections (fold B). Turn the page over and, with the metallic side up, make a diagonal fold corner to corner (fold C). See Fig.1. Bring corners D and E together to create the folded page. The closed corner of the folded page is the spine edge of your page (Fig.2).

2. Glue all the pages together with the folded corners, the spine edges, on top of each other. Clamp to hold while drying. When the glue has dried, the pages will form a metallic star when opened (Fig.3).
3. Add any lettering to the bond paper side of the paper pages at this time.
4. Cover the front and back cover boards with the decorative paper.
5. With the covers right side down on your work surface, glue in the ribbon for the spine and the closure tie as shown in Fig. 4.
6. Glue the pages into the covers with the spine edge of the pages aligned with the spine of the covers. Clamp to hold while drying.
7. Add a charm or seal to the front for further embellishment. ∞

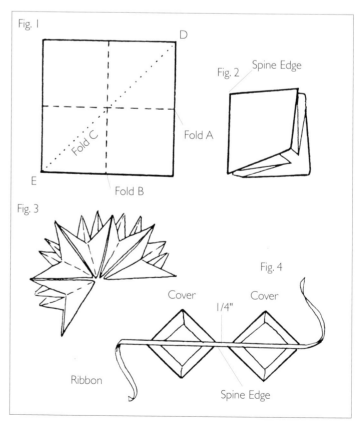

Fig. 1

D

Fold C

Fold A

E

Fold B

Fig. 2 Spine Edge

Fig. 3

Fig. 4

Cover   Cover

1/4"

Ribbon

Spine Edge